PRAYERS FOR ALL THE FAMILY

By the same author:
For All the Family
More For All the Family
Teaching the Families
Reaching the Families
Family Worship
Twenty Questions on Baptism

Prayers For All the Family

COMPILED BY MICHAEL BOTTING

KINGSWAY PUBLICATIONS
EASTBOURNE

First published 1993

ISBN 0 85476 280 9 (paperback)
ISBN 0 85476 378 3 (cased)

Printed in Great Britain for
KINGSWAY PUBLICATIONS LTD
Lottbridge Drove, Eastbourne, E Sussex BN23 6NT by
Clays Ltd, St. Ives plc.
Typeset by J&L Composition Ltd, Filey, North Yorkshire

Dedication

This book is dedicated to the family church of St Michael, Plas Newton, Chester, where my wife Mary and I received such a warm, loving Christian welcome when we moved to our nearby retirement home in 1990; and where I am now privileged to be Honorary Assistant Minister. Some of the material contained in this and other books of mine has had an airing during worship at St Michael's, and some of the prayers are from the children there.

Contents

Foreword

'It works!' was the satisfied comment I received from our four-year-old on meeting her from school one afternoon. On enquiring, 'What works?' I was told (in a voice that indicated it was obvious and I should have known anyway), 'Well, I prayed that I wouldn't be frightened on the climbing-frame, and I wasn't.' The simple direct prayer of a four-year-old and, I believe, God's answer, brings prayer delightfully alive and relevant. We know this to be true and we have proved it over and over again, yet we need constantly to be brought back to a naturalness and freshness in prayer. It is, therefore, a privilege to write this foreword for Michael Botting's book, which is a book for everyone who takes prayer seriously, as well as for those whose praying needs encouragement and help. *Prayers For All the Family* is a rich resource book for every Christian and a useful tool for parents, teachers and all who lead in public worship.

If we are honest, it is strangely difficult when sitting in the congregation, *really* to pray with those who are leading the prayers. So we need to encourage everything that will make this part of the service a time of real prayer for every member of the congregation. This very practical book comes out of years of experience with family services in different churches, but also, and equally importantly, out of experience in parenthood and in taking school assemblies.

As a mother, grandmother and teacher, I appreciate the collects which have been sensitively adapted for children. These should make real prayer easier for them and, I believe, arresting for adults too.

7

Maybe I could add that children would pray with even more understanding if they could read the words themselves from a service sheet or by the use of an overhead projector. As a member of many congregations I would encourage those who lead worship in our churches to make full use of the sensitive and practical advice, as well as the wealth of prayers and litanies in the first section of the book.

The monthly cycle of 'Family Prayers at Home' with Bible readings is an interestingly different idea for family prayers. We used a variety of books and booklets for our children, sharing with them when they were little and then providing for them when they took over their own times of prayer. However, there is always the need for variety with children and I am sure some parents will find in the monthly cycle and helpful prayers which Michael suggests a useful resource.

I would have appreciated the 'Prayers at School Assemblies' section when I was teaching. It is full of interesting and helpful ideas and appropriate prayers for the different age groups. There is the picking up and using of some clever ideas for themes; for example, loneliness, the tongue, bonfires and April Fools' Day, as well as important areas to cover today like All Hallows' Day when the warped ideas of Hallowe'en have now become so strongly 'celebrated'. Again to pick up on Remembrance Day and use that is an excellent teaching opportunity, and yet can be difficult to handle.

Obviously different parts of the book will appeal to different people, but I believe it should enable more of us who belong to Christ and for whom prayer is important, to say quietly in our hearts each day, 'It works!'

Myrtle Baughen

Introduction

No genuine Christians would question the need to pray, though many would admit that regular praying is one of the more difficult parts of their Christian lives. For that reason we cannot start too early. My wife and I began prayers with our children over their cots, so there was never a time in their lives when they were not aware of our praying. When we asked our daughter in her late teens when she first came to faith, she said there was never a time when she did not believe in Jesus.

When the church entered on an almost universal Decade of Evangelism, the emphasis constantly, and rightly, was made that for it to have any chance of being effective it must be *local*. Surely the same is true of prayer. If our children are to learn to pray, then they must experience prayer in their church, home and school.

There are, of course, scores of books on the market about prayer, so readers might well ask what has guided me in the planning, selection and writing of the prayers that follow.

First, I have attempted to make the language lie midway between *The Times* and *The Sun* readership, and although the prayers are for families and not just for children, I have tried to think how a child would understand a particular word, phrase or sentence. For example, I have more often used the name Jesus for the second Person of the Trinity rather than his title Christ, as this is more helpful to the imagination. I have also attempted to avoid sexist language, though I have allowed 'mankind', because 'personkind' seems to highlight

9

the issue rather than play it down. As the book is intended to conform to the teaching of holy Scripture all references to God are masculine.

Secondly, I have attempted to gather prayers from as wide a sphere as possible, including children themselves. More often than not, when responsible for leading a Family Service, I have asked a family to take the intercessions. On quite a number of occasions this has meant that not only did the children share in reading the prayers, but they had also written them too, and usually very well indeed. With the kind help of the Church Pastoral Aid Society, a letter from me requesting original prayers from those under thirteen was circulated to churches on its mailing list in the summer of 1991, and the results will be found throughout this book. Every prayer was accompanied by a letter from a parent confirming that the prayer was original and the writer under thirteen. Some of the prayers received were from young people over that age limit, and the themes for their prayers influenced me in the choice of prayers for the school section.

Thirdly, it will be obvious that I have compiled Section 1 with the Anglican Parish Church in mind. This is partly because I write as a cradle Anglican, and partly because I have been somewhat involved with the Family Service movement in the Church of England over the past thirty years and have been appalled at times over what has passed as a Family Service. The report by the Liturgical Commission of the General Synod, *Patterns for Worship* (Church House Publishing, 1989), voices some of these as early as page 2, under the heading of 'Family' Services. I summarise: childish; banal; too free to be identifiably Anglican; too focused on the nuclear family to the exclusion of the single, bereaved, divorced and elderly; no 'bridge' to more mature worship and often too dominated by the whim of the leader, with little or no consultation with the PCC.

I am concerned that the prayer sections of Family Services should have a more ordered shape and balanced content. I hope the wide variety of reasonably simple, short and direct prayers in this section will help correct some of the failings of the past. Of course in this I am building on what I, with others, sought to do in *Family Worship* (CPAS, 1971, revised edition 1975), which I edited, and Michael Perry and others continued to do in *Church Family Worship* (Hodder & Stoughton, 1986). Some material from each of those publications is repeated here, with appropriate permission where necessary. Despite the Anglican bias in this section, I hope those from a non-Anglican background will still find the material of some value. I am not aware of a similar bias in the remaining sections.

Although divided into three completely separate sections, I trust that the prayers in any one section (e.g. home or church) might be suitable for use elsewhere (e.g. school).

Corporate prayer was encouraged directly by Jesus when he gave us what we normally call the Lord's Prayer, and when he assured us of his specific presence when two or three come together in his name (Matthew 18:20). As to the appropriateness of having previously written prayers, Jesus would have certainly heard special prayers recited at various times in his home and in his local synagogue, and used such prayers himself. The prayer he taught his own disciples, 'Our Father . . .', has the marks of the rabbinical method of teaching, with its careful structure of three petitions for human needs following three for God's glory. It is the type of instruction that would be repeated with the disciples until it was fixed in their memories, much as repeated chorus singing today fixes many popular short Christian songs in ours. I hope and pray that through regular use many of the prayers included in this book will become memorable, and so be easily recalled in time of need.

The other observation I would like to mention concerning our Lord's teaching on prayer is the need to be *specific*. For example, in the parable of the friend who needs help at midnight his request is very specifically for three loaves (Luke 11:5). This definiteness of what we need is usually conspicuously absent in our general intercessions in normal church services, yet we are surely at least two or three gathered in the Lord's name, and are not likely to disagree with the requests made. The Revd David Winter made this point in the *Church Times* diary for 16th August 1991. He was commenting generally favourably on a morning service he had heard recently on Radio 4. 'But,' he continued, 'the intercessions raised a problem that occasionally troubles me. A layman invited us to pray for "the people of Asia"—just like that. Well, I have no objection in principle, but *all* of them? And all at once? And if so many, why not go the whole hog and pray for the entire human race? At least then no one would have cause to feel left out.'

By contrast, I well recall when I was Vicar of St George's, Leeds, I had been informed just before our morning worship began that a small child, whose parents were active members of our congregation, had been admitted to the infirmary next door and was seriously ill. We specifically prayed for her before our worship began. Her healing was reckoned to have begun from that very hour.

I am, of course, extremely indebted to all those who have contributed to this book, not least to the children whose prayers I have been so pleased to include. I should also like to say how especially delighted I am that Myrtle Baughen has written the Foreword. Not only has she three grown-up children and several grandchildren, but she also shares very actively in the exacting ministry of her husband Michael, Bishop of Chester, who has himself written and spoken most helpfully on the subject of prayer.

Dr John Stott, in his book *The Message of Thessalonians* (IVP, 1991, p. 125), writes that he sometimes wonders 'if the comparatively slow progress towards world peace, world equity and world evangelization is not due, more than anything else, to the prayerlessness of the people of God'.

May such prayerlessness not be true of the rising generation, but may we, whether ministers, parents or teachers, be examples to the young, and mean business with God when we come together to worship him—and when we pray in our homes and schools.

May this collection of prayers contribute to that end.

Michael Botting

Section I

PRAYERS IN FAMILY WORSHIP

I

Guidelines for Those Leading Family Services

Apart from the confessions, the contents of this section consist of different kinds of prayer that can be used in the main period of thanksgiving and intercession in the Family Service. It is very important that this time does not become one of 'shuffling boredom', as one writer described it. Most ministers rarely have to sit in the pews with a young family, apart from when on holiday, and so may not be aware of what a difficult time this part of the service can be for most parents. The ABCD of prayer must be applied:

Audibility. If there is the slightest chance that those leading the prayers will not be heard, then a microphone system must be employed, otherwise only those with very good voices should be used. In some small rural churches where microphones may be a rarity, it is possible to use a reel-to-reel tape recorder and microphone as a makeshift amplifier, by having the record and pause buttons both on, and adjusting the volume control so that there is no feedback.

Because of the importance of being heard it will probably be undesirable to have a person leading prayers from the back of the church, or various people leading from their pews. If children in a family are praying, then it is vital that the height of the microphone is quickly adaptable so that the child speaks straight into it.

Brevity. The prayers used should be short, and there should not be too many of them. Though there may be a place for an occasional extempore prayer, there is always a danger that this type of prayer can go on too long, quite apart from lapsing into the 'language of Zion'! If silence is used, it must be very short.

Clarity. By this I not only mean that there should be no misunderstanding of what the prayer is about, but that directions about the prayer time are clear. For example, posture for prayer should be stated: sitting may be particularly desirable for small children, and therefore for everyone. In one church I have attended I think if I adopted the option of kneeling I would be there still! If prayers are to be said together, be sure everyone knows where the prayers are to be found. If litanies are used (i.e. prayers with responses from the congregation), make sure that everyone knows when a response is to be made. If the whole printed litany could be in everyone's hands, better still. If silence is being used, make clear what people should be doing with it, such as remembering personal friends in need.

Diversity. Not only have a variety of types of prayer, as implied above, but have a change of voice. For that reason there is much to be said for having a family to pray. When I did this at a televised service some years ago, this was one of the things that received much comment in the considerable amount of correspondence that followed. Obviously the family should be well briefed with reasonable notice. Children should be encouraged to pray, possibly writing their own prayers. However, you should make it clear that attending a Family Service does not mean that a family will be obliged at some stage to lead the prayers, or some families may be discouraged from attending. On the other hand encourage as many different families as possible to take part from time to time—some may have to be very carefully wooed into doing it. This might be done initially by providing them with the prayers typed out, then by offering them a selection to choose from, and hopefully then reaching the stage where they don't need nannying from you. As a general rule I would avoid using the vicarage or manse family—unless there is a special occasion when it is appropriate—but rather keeping them for the emergency. It is quite a useful practice to have a strong piece of card with directions for leading prayers at a Family Service clearly typed out. The following directions are recommended for Anglican churches; non-conformists will need to make appropriate adjustments:

—The leader of the Family Service will call you up to lead the prayers immediately after the Creed.

—Please stand along the chancel step, the person in charge of leading the prayers making sure that the microphone is always in front of the person praying.

—Begin with the Family Prayer (Lord's Prayer) together. This could be followed with a modern version of the Collect appointed for the particular Sunday or Festival.

—Prepare three or four other prayers. [Mention where suitable prayers for a Family Service can be found, such as in *Prayers For All the Family*.] Make sure that any major news topic is covered as well as the local needs of the parish. Remember too that not everyone present belongs to a nuclear family, so an occasional prayer for the lonely, the single parent, etc may be suitable. Possibly end with a prayer for families and homes and/or the Grace.

Church Family Worship Resource Book gives some valuable advice to those who lead Family Services:

While others are leading prayers, it is important that you yourself are seen to pray; folk will take their lead from you. It may be acceptable to use the first few seconds of the prayer time to sort out your order of service, but no longer.

During the prayers, while praying yourself, you need to keep alert and in touch with what is happening. If there is a gap because someone hasn't turned up or has forgotten the order of things, you can conduct the prayers through eye contact and a nod to each leader (p. 28).

Prayers in a Family Communion Service

It is not my general practice to lead Eucharistic Family Services, but there are special occasions, such as Christmas and Easter Day, when it is appropriate to make exceptions. My custom has been to use the CPAS Family Worship Service, but to follow the lesson with the sermon, possibly with a hymn or chorus one side or the other, or both. Then continue with the Creed and the prayers, but get the leader of these to end with the prayer of humble access from ASB Rite A. Members of the congregation who do not wish to stay for the Communion can leave during the offertory hymn, having had all the main ingredients of a Family Service. Those who stay will have moved into the Communion Service without the join being too conspicuous.

2

Simplified Collects for the Church's Year

The prayers that follow keep to the themes of the Alternative Service Book Collects. Where they are unattributed they are based on *Collects with the New Lectionary* by the Revds Peter Akehurst and Anthony Bishop, first published by Grove Books 1972 and used in their adapted form by permission.

Ninth Sunday before Christmas

1 Lord God,
    you have created the whole universe of stars and planets;
    you have made the world we live on,
    and you have made men and women to look after it.
    Help us to remember that it is your world,
    help us to be grateful for it,
    and help us to use all your gifts in the right way;
    through Jesus Christ our Lord.   Amen.

Eighth Sunday before Christmas

2 Lord God,
    you know our weakness and our naughtiness;
    your Son lived and died and rose again
        to break the power of evil.
Give us the strength to turn away from all that is wrong,

and to become daily more like Jesus.
We ask this in his name.   Amen.

Seventh Sunday before Christmas

3 Lord God,
    you always keep your promises.
Give us a faith like Abraham's,
that we may trust those promises
    and receive the good things
        which you have in store for us,
through Jesus Christ our Lord.   Amen.

Sixth Sunday before Christmas

4 Lord, you have the power
    to rescue us from sin and give us new life,
    just as, through your servant Moses,
        you rescued your people Israel out of slavery in Egypt.
Set us and all people free
    from everything that holds us captive.
Deliver us from the grip of sin and the fear of death,
that we may all rejoice in perfect liberty,
    through Jesus Christ our Lord.   Amen.

Fifth Sunday before Christmas

5 God, our Father,
    you have called your people out of every nation,
        to bear witness to your truth among all people.
Keep us faithful and obedient,
    however few we may be,
    however weak we may feel,
that your will may be fully done in the world,
    through Jesus Christ our Lord.   Amen.

Advent Sunday (Fourth Sunday before Christmas)

6 God of all power,
    the day of your final victory
        will dawn when people least expect it.
    Help us to give up the way of life which belongs to darkness
        and to take up arms as soldiers of the light,
    that we may prepare ourselves in this life
        to rise to be with Jesus when he returns as King.   Amen.

7 Lord Jesus, we thank you for your promise to return to this
world, not as a tiny baby but as a triumphant King. Keep us
watchful against temptation and joyous in your service, for your
name's sake.   Amen.

(Family Worship)

Advent 2 (Third Sunday before Christmas, known as Bible Sunday)

8 We praise you, loving Father,
    that the Bible was written to teach us about you.
    Help us to listen to it, study it and take it to heart,
    so that, as we are strengthened by your word,
        we may have a firm and lasting faith
            in your promise of life in Jesus Christ our Saviour.   Amen.

9 Heavenly Father, through the Bible you have shown the wonder
of your love for us in Jesus Christ. Help us to understand it
with our minds and apply it in our lives, for his sake.   Amen.

(Family Worship)

Advent 3 (Second Sunday before Christmas)

10 Lord Jesus, you sent your servant John the Baptist ahead of you,
    to prepare people for your first coming.
    Help the ministers of your gospel today
        to make people ready for you,

by bringing them to faith and obedience;
that when you come to judge the world
    your people may be pleasing to you.
    We ask this in your name, living, reigning Lord.   Amen.

Advent 4 (First Sunday before Christmas)

11 Heavenly Father,
        you chose the Virgin Mary
            to be the mother of Jesus our Lord and Saviour.
    As we think of her faith, joy and desire to do your will,
    give us help to follow her example,
        for the sake of Jesus Christ her Son, our Lord.   Amen.

Christmas Eve

12 Almighty God,
        you make us glad with the yearly remembrance
            of the birth of your Son, Jesus Christ.
    Grant that, as we joyfully receive him for our Redeemer,
        we may with sure confidence behold him
        when he shall come to be our Judge;
        who is alive and reigns with you and the Holy Spirit,
        one God, now and for ever.   Amen.

                    (*Alternative Service Book 1980 based on Prayer Book, 1549*)

Christmas Day

13 Lord God, we rejoice at the birth of your Son,
        that he became a human being like us
            to be the Saviour of all people.
    As we have been born again through him
        as your adopted children,
        may we grow in grace from day to day
            and be the messengers of your salvation,
        in the name of Jesus
            who with the Spirit shares your endless glory.   Amen.

14 O God, our Father, we remember the birth of your Son, Jesus Christ, and welcome him with gladness as Saviour. We pray that there may always be room for him in our hearts and in our homes, for his sake.   Amen.

(Family Worship)

Christmas 1

15 Lord Jesus, you came to do your Father's will.
Give us the singleness of mind and dedication
    of heart which you displayed,
that we may rejoice to serve and follow you.
    We ask this in your name.   Amen.

Christmas 2 and Epiphany

16 God of light and power,
    as you led the wise men by a star to worship your Son,
    so bring all nations to see your light in him,
    that the world may be filled with your glory,
        through Jesus Christ our Lord.   Amen.

17 Lord God, we remember how you led the wise men to Bethlehem by the light of a star. Guide us as we travel to the heavenly city that we, and all people, may know Jesus as the true and living way, for his name's sake.   Amen.

(Family Worship, adapted)

Epiphany 1

18 Lord Jesus,
        in your baptism you became one with us sinful people,
        and were revealed there to be the Son of God.
    May we who have been baptised in your name,
        rejoice that we can share your sonship
        and give ourselves in the service of other people.
        We ask this for your glory, living, reigning Lord.   Amen.

Epiphany 2

19 Lord God,
> your Son Jesus Christ called people
> > to deny themselves and follow him.
>
> Give us strength to hand ourselves wholly over to his service
> > and to be lights for him in the world around us.
> > We ask this in his name.   Amen.

Epiphany 3

20 Lord Jesus,
> your power makes new whatever it touches:
> change our sinfulness into your purity,
> that others may see the difference your grace makes
> > to our lives.   Amen.

Epiphany 4

21 God of mercy,
> we praise you that you welcome sinners and forgive them.
> Give us true sorrow for our sins,
> > the knowledge of your pardon,
> > and the assurance of eternal life,
> > > in Jesus Christ our Lord.   Amen.

Epiphany 5

22 Lord God,
> your mercy never fails;
> you bring us new hope and new life;
> without you we are nothing.
> Give us your help in all we do,
> > and keep us always dependent on yourself,
> > through Jesus Christ our Lord.   Amen.

23 Give us, Lord, we pray,
> the spirit to think and to do always

those things that are right:
that we who can do no good thing without you
may have power to live according to your holy will;
through Jesus Christ our Lord.   Amen.

(*Alternative Service Book 1980*)

Epiphany 6

24 Almighty God,
   your Son has opened to us
      a new and living way into your presence.
Give us pure hearts and obedient wills,
that we may worship you in spirit and in truth,
   through Jesus Christ our Lord.   Amen.

Ninth Sunday before Easter (Third before Lent)

25 Lord Jesus Christ,
   you came to teach us the way of life which God requires.
Make us open to your word,
   and help us to obey, whatever it may cost,
that our lives may bear much fruit,
   to the glory of your name.   Amen.

Eighth Sunday before Easter (Second before Lent)

26 Loving Saviour,
   you can heal all our ills
      and deliver us from every kind of trouble.
Make us whole, we pray, both in body and spirit,
that we may be agents of your healing in the world,
      to the glory of your name.   Amen.

Seventh Sunday before Easter (next before Lent)

27 Lord God,
   your power is boundless and will never fail.

Look in mercy on us in our weakness;
protect us in every danger
    and come to our help in every time of need;
    through Jesus Christ our Lord.   Amen.

Ash Wednesday

28 God of everlasting love,
    you care for everything that you have made
    and forgive the sins of all who repent.
Make us truly sorry for our disobedience
    and determined to amend our lives,
that we may receive your pardon, Lord of mercy;
    in the name of Jesus Christ your Son.   Amen.

29 Teach us, good Lord, to serve you as you deserve, to give and
not to count the cost, to fight and not to heed the wounds, to
toil and not to seek for rest, to labour and not to ask for any
reward, except that of knowing that we do your will, through
Jesus Christ our Lord.   Amen.

(Family Worship after St Ignatius Loyola)

Lent 1 (Sixth Sunday before Easter)

30 Lord Jesus Christ,
    you were tempted like us in every way,
    and yet you never sinned.
Bring us strength in our weakness,
that we too may stand firm against temptation;
    to the glory of your name.   Amen.

Lent 2 (Fifth Sunday before Easter)

31 Lord Jesus, Conqueror of Satan,
drive him out of our hearts;
fill us with your Holy Spirit;
equip us against every spiritual enemy;
that we may live to your glory.   Amen.

Lent 3 (Fourth Sunday before Easter)

32 Lord God,
     your Son had to suffer
       before he could be glorified.
  Make us willing to deny ourselves
     and follow in his footsteps,
  that we may come to share his joy.   Amen.

Lent 4 (Third Sunday before Easter, also Mothering Sunday)

33 God of all might,
     you revealed the glory of your Son
       to his disciples on the mountain.
  May we reflect his glory
     in the power of your Spirit,
  and so be changed into his likeness
     for the sake of Jesus Christ our Lord.   Amen.

34 O Lord, thank you for our mothers and for all they do for us.
Be close to them when they are tired with housework, and help
us always to love them and do all we can to help them in our
home. Through Jesus Christ our Lord.   Amen.

(Family Worship)

Lent 5 (Second Sunday before Easter)

35 Lord Jesus,
     you defeated the powers of evil by your death,
       and set us free by the shedding of your blood.
  Give us a firm faith in your sacrifice,
  that we may share in your victory
     and bring glory to your name.   Amen.

Palm Sunday (Sunday before Easter)

36 Loving Father,
     you sent your Son to become a person like us

and to die for us on the cross,
like a lamb led to the slaughter.
May we know the greatness of his saving power over sin
and follow his example of humility.
We ask this in his name.   Amen.

37 As you entered your city of Jerusalem and your temple, O Lord,
so enter into our hearts and minds this day. Help us to welcome
you with truth and with sincerity and teach us to walk in your
way all the days of our life; through the same Jesus Christ our
Lord.   Amen.

(*Adapted from a prayer from More Prayers for Today's Church*)

Good Friday

38 Jesus, our Saviour,
you suffered a cruel death
and the pain of separation from your Father,
to bring us back to him.
Draw us nearer to yourself;
deepen our understanding of your love;
fill our hearts with thankfulness.
We ask this in your name, living, reigning Lord.   Amen.

39 Heavenly Father, we thank you for giving your Son to die on
the cross that we might be forgiven. Help us to understand the
consequences of our sin and the greatness of his love, so that
we may trust him as our Saviour and serve him as our
Lord.   Amen.

(*Family Worship*)

Easter Eve

40 As you died for us, Lord Jesus,
may we die to ourselves;
may the sinful part of us be buried with you,
and may we also rise with you
to new life by the Father's power.   Amen.

Easter Day

41 Lord God, you raised your Son in triumph from the grave,
    conquering the power of sin and death,
    and opening the way to eternal life for all people.
Unite us with him in his risen life,
    to serve you joyfully in his strength
    and to bring the news of his victory to others,
that the world may be filled with his glory.   Amen.

42 Lord Jesus, our risen Saviour, we rejoice in your mighty victory
over sin and death. You are the Prince of life, you are alive for
ever more. Help us to know your presence, not only as we
worship you here, but at home, and at work, and wherever we
go; for your great name's sake.   Amen.

(Family Worship)

Easter 1

43 Almighty God,
    you have given us the Bread of Life
    in your Son Jesus Christ.
We pray that we may feed on him,
    our risen, living Lord,
and so enjoy true life, now and for ever.   Amen.

Easter 2

44 Good Shepherd,
    we praise you for your love and protection of your people.
    Keep us always in that love;
    make us sure of that protection
    that we may follow you wherever you may lead,
        to the glory of your name.   Amen.

Easter 3

45 Lord God,
     you raised your Son from death
     to be the resurrection and the life for all believers.
Raise us to true life in him,
and set our hearts and minds on heavenly things,
that we may be ready to share his glory
     when he comes in power.   Amen.

Easter 4

46 Almighty God,
     you have given us your Son Jesus Christ
          to be the way, the truth and the life;
          the one by whom we come to you.
Help us in faith to follow him,
     as your apostles did,
     and to do the work you have for us to do;
     through Jesus Christ our Lord.   Amen.

Easter 5

47 Lord Jesus Christ,
     you returned to the glory of your Father,
     that you might send us your Spirit
          to be with us for ever.
May we know his presence and power in our lives,
     and be guided into all truth.
     We ask this in your name.   Amen.

Ascension Day

48 Jesus, King of the universe, thank you for rising to the Father's
throne on high to take control of all things.
Help us to trust you when life is difficult and obey you at all
times. We ask this for the honour of your name.   Amen.

(Family Worship)

49 All praise to you, Sovereign Lord,
    for your Son's ascension in triumph
        to rule in glory over all creation.
    Bring all mankind to recognise him as Lord
        and to do his will,
    that you may be glorified on earth
        as you are in heaven.   Amen.

The Sunday after Ascension Day

50 Almighty God,
    your Son ascended to the throne of power in heaven,
    that he might be Lord over all things for his people.
    We pray that the worship and service of the church
        may be inspired by his presence,
        and that he will remain with us always,
            to the end of the age.   Amen.

Pentecost (Whitsunday)

51 Father,
    you sent your Holy Spirit to your people
        to give them power and boldness
        to be your witnesses to all nations.
    Fill us with his power,
        and send us out to bring the world to you;
        through Jesus Christ our Lord.   Amen.

52 We praise you, O God, because you gave the Holy Spirit to
    the first Christians, making Jesus real to them, teaching them
    the truth and giving them power to witness boldly. Fill us with
    the same Spirit that we may know their experience and follow
    their example, for Jesus' sake.   Amen.

                                                    (*Family Worship*)

Trinity Sunday (Pentecost 1)

53 God our Father,
        you have provided for all our needs,
            in our Saviour Jesus Christ.
    Make us faithful and obedient servants,
    that in the strength of your Spirit
        we may live for your glory in the service of others;
        through Jesus Christ our Lord.   Amen.

54 Almighty and eternal God,
    you have revealed yourself
        as Father, Son, and Holy Spirit,
    and live and reign in the perfect unity of love.
    Hold us firm in this faith,
    that we may know you in all your ways
    and evermore rejoice in your eternal glory,
    who are three Persons in one God,
    now and for ever.   Amen.

(Alternative Service Book 1980)

Pentecost 2 (Trinity 1)

55 Lord,
        you have chosen men and women to be the agents
            of your purpose in the world.
    Bind us together;
    enable us to grow up into Jesus;
    help us to proclaim to others your saving grace;
        in the name and by the power of Jesus Christ.   Amen.

Pentecost 3 (Trinity 2)

56 Almighty God,
        we thank you for bringing us to new life in Jesus,
            signed and sealed in baptism.
    May we live as new people in him,

and in love and freedom bear witness
      to his risen life;
through Christ our Lord.   Amen.

Pentecost 4 (Trinity 3)

57 Eternal God,
      you plan that people should live
      in freedom as your sons and daughters.
    Draw all mankind into the freedom of your family,
    that the divisions of peoples and nations
      may be overcome in the love of your Son,
          our Saviour Jesus Christ.   Amen.

Pentecost 5 (Trinity 4)

58 Lord,
      you have commanded us to love one another.
    Free us from love of self,
      and teach us to love all people for your sake;
        through Jesus Christ our Lord.   Amen.

Pentecost 6 (Trinity 5)

59 God, the Creator and Redeemer of mankind,
      renew us in the image of your Son,
    fill us with his love,
    let his peace dwell in our hearts,
    that all we do may be for him, who gave himself for us,
      Jesus Christ our Lord.   Amen.

Pentecost 7 (Trinity 6)

60 Lord of love,
      forgive our failure to love,
      give us your love,
      and love others through us;
        in the name and by the power of Jesus Christ.   Amen.

Pentecost 8 (Trinity 7)

61 Lord Jesus,
> you chose your disciples to bear fruit
> > that should last.
> By the power of your Spirit
> make us fruitful in your service.
> We ask this in your name.   Amen.

Pentecost 9 (Trinity 8)

62 Lord God,
> you call us to take our place in the warfare of faith.
> Arm us, we pray, with spiritual weapons;
> train us in their use.
> And help us to defeat evil in the world and in ourselves;
> > by the victory of Jesus our Saviour.   Amen.

Pentecost 10 (Trinity 9)

63 Almighty God,
> in Jesus you humbled yourself and took the form of a servant.
> Let this mind be in us,
> that we may show forth your love
> > in caring for the needy and distressed
> > and by humbly serving one another;
> > to the glory of your name.   Amen.

Pentecost 11 (Trinity 10)

64 Lord God Almighty,
> you came to live as a servant among mankind.
> Take from us all false ideas of greatness.
> Make us one in your service of others,
> that in the fellowship of your church
> > we may become the willing servants of all;
> > for Jesus' sake.   Amen.

Pentecost 12 (Trinity 11)

65 Father,

you have committed to men and women
    the good news of your saving love
    and set us as ambassadors for Jesus in your world.
Help us together to bear witness to the message of the forgiveness
    of sins,
that in the life of your church people may become new creatures
    in Jesus Christ our Lord.   Amen.

Pentecost 13 (Trinity 12)

66 Lord Jesus,

you suffered on the cross for our salvation.
Help us to understand the mystery of your pain,
    to accept patiently our share of suffering,
    and to enter with compassion into the sufferings of others.
    We ask this in your name.   Amen.

Pentecost 14 (Trinity 13)

67 Lord God,

you came as neighbour to mankind in Jesus.
Give us eyes to see you in other people,
    and make us instruments of your care to all,
that everyone may become true neighbours
    in Jesus Christ our Lord.   Amen.

Pentecost 15 (Trinity 14)

68 God our Father,

you set each of us within the life of a human family.
Bless, we pray, the families of mankind;
unite us in mutual care and support;
give us right standards of truth, obedience and respect,
and help us to grow in awareness and understanding;
    through Jesus Christ our Lord.   Amen.

Pentecost 16 (Trinity 15)

69 Almighty and eternal God,
guide those who bear authority in the nations of the world;
relieve those who suffer oppression and exploitation;
lead us in justice and freedom;
show us how to use our resources to serve the good of all;
    through Jesus Christ our Lord.　Amen.

Pentecost 17 (Trinity 16)

70 Lord,
    you command us to hear your word and obey it.
Help us to put our faith into action,
that your kingdom may come and your will be done
    on earth as in heaven.　Amen.

Pentecost 18 (Trinity 17)

71 Lord our Saviour,
    you became poor to make us rich.
Give us grace to serve you with all that we possess,
that our lives may be a willing sacrifice
    of love and praise to you.
    We ask this in your name.　Amen.

Pentecost 19 (Trinity 18)

72 Lord,
    you call men and women to live by faith.
Enable us in faith to respond to your call,
and in the fellowship of your church
    to grow in trust and commitment;
    to the glory of your Son Jesus Christ.　Amen.

Pentecost 20 (Trinity 19)

73 Loving Father,
   you desire your people
      to live on earth as citizens of heaven.
   Keep us steadfast in this calling,
   that through us men and women may come to share
      the peace of your kingdom;
      for Jesus' sake.   Amen.

Pentecost 21 (Trinity 20)

74 Lord of all faithfulness,
   you have enabled men and women through faith
      to enter into glory.
   Give us strength to endure
      and to follow Jesus the whole way to our salvation;
      for the glory of your name.   Amen.

Pentecost 22 (Trinity 21)

75 God of glory,
   you have made us to share through Jesus
      the mystery of worship with the hosts of heaven and all
      creation.
   Give us reality in our worship,
   that we may acknowledge you in reverence and sincerity
      and work for justice and freedom among all people;
         through Jesus Christ our Lord.   Amen.

Pentecost 23 (Trinity 22)

76 God of peace,
   you call men and women to repentance
   and have graciously met their needs in a new agreement with
      yourself.

Give us true sorrow for our sin;
enable us to fulfil the ministry you set before us;
make us holy in every part of our being;
    through Jesus Christ our Lord.   Amen.

3

Confessions

77 Almighty God, we confess that we have sinned against you in thought, word and deed: we have not loved you with all our heart; we have not loved our neighbours as ourselves. Have mercy upon us: cleanse us from our sins; and help us to overcome our faults: through Jesus Christ our Lord.   Amen.

(Family Worship)

78 *Minister:* If we say we have no sin, we deceive ourselves, and the truth is not in us.

All: If we confess our sins, God is faithful and just to forgive us our sins and cleanse us from every kind of wrong.
Father, have mercy on us and forgive us,
through Jesus Christ our Lord.   Amen.

(Based on 1 John 1:8–9—adapted from Family Worship)

79 *Minister:* We will arise and go to our Father and will say to him:

All: Father, we have sinned against heaven and before you and are no more worthy to be called your children. Forgive us and help us, through the name of our Saviour, Jesus Christ.   Amen.

(Based on Luke 15:18–19)

80 Merciful Lord, grant to your faithful people pardon and peace:
    that we may be cleansed from all our sins and serve you with
    a quiet mind; through Jesus Christ our Lord.   Amen.

(The Alternative Service Book 1980 Collect of seventh Sunday before Easter)

81 O God, our loving Father, we confess that we have sinned against
    you and done many things to grieve you. We have often been
    selfish and ill-tempered, and disobedient. We have sometimes
    forgotten to pray to you, and we have not loved you as we
    ought. For these and all our other sins, loving Father, forgive
    us, for the sake of him who died for us, Jesus Christ our
    Lord.   Amen.

*(Michael Botting, adapted from the Confession in the Family Service at St Matthew's
Church, Fulham, 1963)*

82 Lord Jesus Christ, crucified, risen and ascended for us:
    we have not loved you as our Redeemer, nor obeyed you as our
        Lord;
    we have not brought our prayers to you,
    nor heeded your tears shed over the world.
    Forgive us, we pray;
    breathe into us a new spirit of service,
    and make us joyfully obedient to your will;
    for your glory's sake.   Amen.

(Michael Perry—Church Family Worship 288)

83 O God, our gracious Father,
    we confess that we have sinned against you
    and done many things to grieve you.
    We have often been selfish,
    we have sometimes forgotten to pray to you,
    and we have not loved you as we should.
    For these and all other sins forgive us, we pray,
    through him who died for us, Jesus Christ our Lord.   Amen.

(C.S. Woodward, adapted from The Children's Service)

84 Dear Father, sorry for all the naughty things I've done, said or
        thought.

Please take my hand and guide me into your love and care, and work in my life to make me the person you want me to be.   Amen.

(Emma Ruth Baldock, Rotherham, aged 5)

(The above confession is used at Brampton Church, Rotherham, during the baptisms of young children who are old enough to make promises for themselves.)

85 O God, you made us and you love us. Thank you for being so willing to forgive us. Make us quick to own up to you whenever we do wrong so that we may quickly be forgiven. Then our day will not be spoilt by worry and we can be happy all day long; through Jesus Christ our Lord.   Amen.

(Dick Williams)

86 *Minister:*

All of us sometimes fail to do the things we should.

All of us sometimes say and do things we know to be wrong.

Let us tell God how sorry we are, and ask him to forgive us.

[*pause*]

All (led by Minister): O search me, God, and know my heart.

O test me and know my thoughts.

See that I follow not the wrong path,

and lead me in the path of life eternal.

[*pause*]

All (led by Minister): O God, our loving Father,

we know that you forgive those who honestly confess their sins.

We pray you to forgive us

for the good things we have failed to do,

and for the wrong things we have done.

We have often broken your rules.

We have often forgotten what Jesus said.

All these things we confess to you.

We ask your forgiveness,

and we ask you to help us live better
lives day by day,
for Jesus Christ's sake.   Amen.

(Anon—central section from Psalm 139: 23–24)

A confession for use on Mothering Sunday (Fourth in Lent)

87 Almighty God, we confess that we have sinned against you in
thought, word and deed. We are especially sorry for the many
times when we have taken our homes for granted and have made
our mother's work more difficult by our selfishness and bad
temper, our unkindness and thoughtlessness. Have mercy upon
us, cleanse us from our sins and help us to overcome our faults;
through Jesus Christ our Lord.   Amen.

(Family Worship, adapted)

*(There are litanies of confession, including one especially for Harvest, in
Section 1, Chapter 5.)*

4

Thanksgivings

General thanksgivings

88 Our Lord God, we thank you for all your blessings, for life and
health, for laughter and fun, for all powers of mind and body,
for our homes and the love of dear ones, for everything that is
beautiful, good and true; but above all for giving your Son to
be our Saviour and Friend. May we always find our true happiness
in pleasing you and helping others to know and love
you.   Amen.

(Family Worship)

89 Thank you for our family, thank you for our friends;
thank you for such love, dear Lord, that never ever ends.
Thank you for the sunshine, thank you for the rain;
thank you for your love, dear Lord, that suffered for sin's pain.
Thank you for the cross, dear Lord. We're sorry it had to be.
Thank you for the promise, Lord, that one day you we'll
    see.   Amen.

(Slightly adapted from a prayer by Colin Ross, Ayr, aged 11)

90 Dear Jesus,
    thank you for food you give us to eat,
    thank you for our pet animals,
    thank you for all babies,

thank you for mums and dads, and brothers and sisters,
thank you for teachers at our school,
thank you, Jesus, for everyone.   Amen.

(Claire McMillan, Croydon, aged 6)

91 Dear Lord, thank you for all that you have given us; for money
and light, for houses and clothes, for food and drink, trees and
plants, for paper and paint, for books and especially the Bible.
Thank you, God.   Amen.

(Based on ideas from Sean Bowles, Leicester, aged 8)

For the wonders of creation

92 Dear Father God, thank you for all the animals in your world.
Even the biggest to the smallest animals, you made them all.
Thank you, God, for the little rabbits with their happy little
hops and the birds with their little beaks that help them sing
all day.
Please help us to look after all the animals in the world and
keep them safe, even those that we think may hurt us.   Amen.

(Lisa Clements, Croydon, aged 9)

93 Dear God, thank you for your wonderful world, for the animals
that roam around, for flowers and trees that bloom every year,
for creepy crawlies that crawl around.
Help us not to pollute your world. Teach us to look after it so
that it can be shared by everyone.   Amen.

(Richard Kennett, Stroud, aged 9)

For Harvest

94 Dear Lord, thank you for the harvest, both from the land and
from the sea. But help us, Lord, not to forget the people of the
third world, but share our riches with them:
food, that they will not starve,
machines, that will make their water clean,
doctors and nurses, to help them to be healthy.

We ask this for Jesus' sake.   Amen.

(Based on ideas provided by children from Richard Hill Primary School {Church of England—Aided}, Thurcaston, Leicester, 1991)

For Jesus

95 Dear Father, we thank you for the wonderful life of Jesus; for his strength and energy, for his gentleness and happiness, for his love and care for everyone, for his remarkable teaching and amazing miracles. But very especially we thank you for his unflinching courage in the face of mockery, torture and death; for the sacrifice he made that our sins might be forgiven. Help us who bear his name to live more nearly as he did.   Amen.

(Michael Botting, based on a prayer by Rupert E. Davies)

For families

96 Heavenly Father, we thank you for our homes and families, for our food and clothing and for all the happiness that parents and children can share. We ask that your love may surround us, your care may protect us, and that we may know your peace at all time; for Jesus' sake.   Amen.

(Family Worship)

For the birth of a child

97 We rejoice before you, Creator God, in all your marvellous works.
We bless you for the miracle of new life, and that you have called men and women to share in this wonder.
Today we especially thank you for the safe delivery of this child [name, if known]; praying that (s)he may grow physically to healthy adulthood, and spiritually to know and love you, whom to know is eternal life, in Jesus Christ our Lord.   Amen.

(Michael Botting)

For friends

98 Dear Lord, thank you for friends, for people who really listen
to us and for people who understand us. Thank you for our
teachers at church and at school. And thank you especially for
Jesus, who helps us to know how we should live our
lives.   Amen.

(Based on ideas from Joel Glover, Leicester, aged 9)

(Further thanksgivings can be found in the next chapter.)

5

Simple Litanies

At the beginning of public worship

99 *Leader:* God our Father, we have come to church this morning/
evening to meet you. We want to speak to you and
listen to what you are saying to us.

   All: Please quieten our minds, and help us to think about
what we are doing.

   Leader: There are things that we are sorry we did, because they
were wrong. There are other things that we did not
do, which we know we should have done.

   All: Please forgive us for our mistakes, and help us not to
make them again.

   Leader: We thank you for life, and for sending Jesus into the
world so that we can enjoy it even more. We are grateful
to you for taking care of us from day to day.

   All: Please accept our thanks, and help us never to take your
love for granted.   Amen.

(Adapted from an unknown source)

The Commandments

100 *Leader:* Our Lord Jesus Christ said:
'You shall love the Lord your God with all your heart,
and with all your soul, and with all your mind, and

with all your strength. This is the first and greatest
commandment.

All: 'And the second is like it: you shall love your neighbour
as yourself.

Leader: 'There is no commandment greater than these.

All: 'On these two commandments depend all the law and
the prophets.'

Leader: May God enable us to do these things, now and always.

All: Amen.

(*Matthew 22:36–40*)

Litanies of confession

101 *Leader:*   Lord God, our Maker and our Redeemer, this is your
world and we are your people: come among us and save
us. Where we have wilfully misused your gifts of
creation, be merciful, Lord:

All: Forgive us and help us.

Leader: Where we have seen the ill-treatment of others and have
not gone to their aid, be merciful, Lord:

All: Forgive us and help us.

Leader: Where we have condoned the lie in our society, and
failed to achieve justice or compassion, be merciful,
Lord:

All: Forgive us and help us.

Leader: Where we have heard for ourselves the good news of
Christ, but have not shared it with our generation nor
taught it to our children, be merciful, Lord:

All: Forgive us and help us.

Leader: Where we have not loved you with all our heart, nor
our neighbours as ourselves, be merciful, Lord:

All: Forgive us and help us.
O God, forgive us for our lack of love, and in your mercy
make us what you would have us be, through Jesus
Christ our Lord.   Amen.

(*Michael Perry, Church Family Worship 51*)

102 *Leader:* Almighty God, our Father, we come to you with humble hearts, to confess our sins.

For turning away from you, and ignoring your will for our lives:

Father, forgive us,

All: save us and help us.

Leader: For behaving just as we wish, without thinking of you: Father, forgive us,

All: save us and help us.

Leader: For failing you—not only by what we do, but also by our thoughts and words: Father, forgive us,

All: save us and help us.

Leader: For letting ourselves be drawn away from you by temptations in the world about us: Father, forgive us,

All: save us and help us.

Leader: For acting as if we were ashamed to belong to your dear Son Jesus: Father, forgive us,

All: save us and help us.

Father, we have failed you often, and humbly ask your forgiveness: help us so to live that others may see your glory; through Jesus Christ our Lord. Amen.

(Michael Perry, Church Family Worship 135)

103 *Leader:* O Jesus Christ, risen Master and triumphant Lord, we come to you in sorrow for our sins, and confess to you our weakness and unbelief.

We have lived by our own strength, and not by the power of your resurrection. In your mercy, forgive us:

All: Lord, hear us and help us.

Leader: We have lived by the light of our own eyes, as faithless and not believing. In your mercy, forgive us:

All: Lord, hear us and help us.

Leader: We have lived for this world alone, and doubted our home in heaven. In your mercy, forgive us:

All: Lord, hear us and help us.

Lift our minds above earthly things, set them on things

above; show us your glory and your power, that we may
serve you gladly all our days.   Amen.

(Michael Perry, Church Family Worship 244)

104 *Leader:*   Almighty God, we confess that we have often misused
and ill-treated your creation: hear us, and in your mercy
save us and help us.

For every act of carelessness that has treated the world
merely as a playground: Father, forgive us—

All: save us and help us.

Leader: For every act of wastefulness that forgets the crying of
the needy: Father, forgive us—

All: save us and help us.

Leader: For every act of selfishness that defies your just rule
over our lives: Father, forgive us—

All: save us and help us.

Cleanse us from our sins through the love of Christ, and
set us free for his service through the power of the Spirit;
for the glory of your name.   Amen.

(Worship Now, St Andrew Press, Church of Scotland)

105 *Leader:*   Let us confess our sins to God and ask for his
forgiveness.

For all the wrong things we have done: in your mercy,

All: forgive us, O God.

Leader: For forgetting what we ought to have remembered, for
failing to do as we promised, for turning away when
we should have listened, for being careless when we
should have been diligent: in your mercy,

All: forgive us, O God.

Leader: For doing things we knew would annoy, for acting in
ways we knew would hurt, for behaving in ways we
knew would disappoint: in your mercy,

All: forgive us, O God.

Leader: O God, when we look back we can see how foolish
and wrong we have been. Forgive us, and help us not

to do the same things again: through Jesus Christ our
Lord. Amen.

(After William Barclay)

106 *Leader:* O God, we come to you in repentance, conscious of
our sins.

When we are self-satisfied, you expose our failure. Lord,
forgive us:

All: save us and help us.

Leader: When we are self-assertive, you challenge our pride.
Lord, forgive us:

All: save us and help us.

Leader: When we are self-opinionated, you show us we do not
know everything. Lord, forgive us:

All: save us and help us.

Leader: When we are self-indulgent, you condemn our greed.
Lord, forgive us:

All: save us and help us.

Leader: When we are self-centred, you take our peace away.
Lord, forgive us:

All: save us and help us. Give us a new vision of your
holiness, make us worthy to be your people, and help
us to live up to our calling in Jesus Christ our
Lord. Amen.

(Author sought, Church Family Worship 465)

At Harvest

107 *Leader:* We confess, O God, that we have often taken your
gifts to us for granted; we have not thanked you for
them and we have sometimes wasted them.

All: We are sorry, holy Lord.

Leader: We have often been selfish and greedy and have not
given to the hungry and needy.

All: We are sorry, holy Lord.

Leader: We have sinned against you in thought, word and
deed, we have not loved you with all our heart or loved
our neighbours as ourselves.

All: We are sorry, holy Lord.

Leader: May God, our heavenly Father, who has promised to
           forgive all those who sincerely turn to him, have mercy
           on each one of you. May he deliver you from your sins,
           selfishness and greed, and strengthen you for his service;
           through Jesus Christ our Lord.   Amen.

                                                    (*Family Worship, revised*)

A litany for life

108 *Leader:*   Let us pray to God our loving Father in penitence and
                faith.

                For needlessly polluting and destroying our
                environment,

All: Father, forgive us.

Leader: For our inhuman treatment of unborn life,

All: Father, forgive us.

Leader: For shamefully neglecting the poor and the sick,

All: Father, forgive us.

             [*Silent pause for reflection*]

Leader: That we may learn to understand and protect your
           creation,

All: Father, help us.

Leader: That we may learn to reverence and respect all human
           life,

All: Father, help us.

Leader: That we may learn to love and care for all who are in
           need,

All: Father, help us.

             [*Silent pause for reflection*]

Leader: Merciful and loving God

All: Hear our prayers through Jesus Christ our
           Lord.   Amen.

                            (*Dick Hines, chaplain and tutor, Oak Hill College, London
                            from The Order of Christian Unity leaflet, 1991*)

Creeds

109 *Leader:* Do you believe and trust in God the Father, who made
the world?

Answer: I believe and trust in him.

Leader: Do you believe and trust in his Son Jesus Christ, who
redeemed mankind?

Answer: I believe and trust in him.

Leader: Do you believe and trust in his Holy Spirit, who gives
life to the people of God?

Answer: I believe and trust in him.

(Alternative Service Book, 1980)

110 *Leader:* Do you believe in God?

People: We believe in God the Father who made us and all the
world.

Leader: Do you believe in Jesus Christ?

People: We believe in Jesus Christ, the Son of God, who came
to this earth to be our Saviour. He died for our sins
on the cross, rose again from the dead, ascended to the
Father in heaven and will come again in his glory as
the Judge of all people.

Leader: Do you believe in the Holy Spirit?

People: We believe in the Holy Spirit, whom God gives to all
who trust in Christ. He makes us more like Jesus,
guides and strengthens us in our daily life, and helps
us serve God in the family of the church.

Leader: May Almighty God strengthen this faith in
us.   Amen.

(Family Worship, adapted to the first person plural)

Litanies of thanksgiving

111 *Leader:* We thank God for giving us other people to be part
of our lives.

For parents, and the love which brought us to birth:
we praise you, O Lord,

All: and bring you thanks today.

Leader: For mothers who have cherished and nurtured us: we praise you, O Lord,

All: and bring you thanks today.

Leader: For fathers who have loved and supported us: we praise you, O Lord,

All: and bring you thanks today.

Leader: For brothers and sisters with whom we have shared our home: we praise you, O Lord,

All: and bring you thanks today.

Leader: For children, entrusted to our care as parents: we praise you, O Lord,

All: and bring you thanks today.

Leader: For other relatives and friends who have been with us in our hopes and our joys: we praise you, O Lord,

All: and bring you thanks today.

Leader: For all who first spoke to us of Jesus, and have drawn us into the family of our Father in heaven: we praise you, O Lord,

All: and bring you thanks today. Help us to live as those who belong to one another and to you, now and always.   Amen.

(Michael Perry, Church Family Worship 197)

112 *Leader:* Let us thank God for all his goodness to us.
For creating the world and for preserving it until now: we give you thanks, O Lord,

All: and praise your holy name.

Leader: For the regular return of day and night, and of the seasons: we give you thanks, O Lord,

All: and praise your holy name.

Leader: For the wonder of nature and the beauty of the earth: we give you thanks, O Lord,

All: and praise your holy name.

Leader: For our memory, which enables us to build on the experience of the past: we give you thanks, O Lord,

All: and praise your holy name.

Leader: For our imagination, which admits us to a wider world than we could otherwise know: we give you thanks, O Lord,

All: and praise your holy name.

Leader: For the grace by which you have revealed yourself to us: we give you thanks, O Lord,

All: and praise your holy name.

Leader: For your patience with our waywardness and your forgiveness for our sinfulness: we give you thanks, O Lord,

All: and praise your holy name.

Leader: Above all we thank you for the promise of all things made new, and for our re-creation in your dear Son, Jesus Christ our Lord.   Amen.

(Contemporary Prayers for Public Worship)

113 *Leader:* Father Almighty, for your majesty and your mercy— loving us still in our waywardness, forgiving us in our unworthiness: we bring you our worship

All: and offer you thanksgiving.

Leader: Jesus, our Redeemer, for your humility and your sacrifice—sharing our joys and our sorrows, dying and rising for our salvation: we bring you our worship

All: and offer you thanksgiving.

Leader: Holy Spirit of God, for your guidance and your encouragement—inspiring and empowering the church, revealing to us all truth: we bring you our worship

All: and offer you thanksgiving.
God of gods—Father, Son and Holy Spirit, eternal Lord, Three-in-One; to you be glory, honour and praise, for ever and ever.   Amen.

(Michael Perry, Church Family Worship 344)

114 *Leader:* Heavenly Father, we come before you with thanksgiving for all your mercy and your grace.
For the beauty of the world around us, we bring you our love,

All: and give you thanks and praise.

Leader: For our parents and our families, we bring you our love,

All: and give you thanks and praise.

Leader: For work and play, for food and clothes, we bring you our love,

All: and give you thanks and praise.

Leader: For the joy of friends, and for the happiness we share, we bring you our love,

All: and give you thanks and praise.

Leader: But most of all, for your Son Jesus Christ, for his wonderful birth, for the example of his life, for his death on the cross to save us, for raising him from the dead to be our living Lord, and for sending upon us your Holy Spirit, we bring you our love,

All: and give you thanks and praise. Help us to serve you gladly and faithfully all our days, until you call us to worship you in heaven.   Amen.

(Emmanuel Church, Northwood)

115 *Leader:*   Praise the Lord, all his works!

All: Praise the Lord, O my soul!

Leader: The heavens declare the glory of the Lord

All: and the earth shows his handiwork.

Leader: For the beauty of the earth and of the sky,
for the sun that warms us,
for the rain that waters the earth,
for the flowers and all the beautiful things around us,
and for the good food that strengthens us

All: we praise you, O God.

Leader: For the songs of the birds,
for music and our power to hear,
for the scent of flowers, and our power to smell,
for the sunsets, for all things of beauty
and our power to see them,

All: we thank you, O God.

Leader: For the love of our parents and friends,
for the kindness and help of other people

All:	we thank you, Lord Jesus.
Leader:	For our health and strength,
	for our powers of mind and body,
All:	We thank you, Lord Jesus.
Leader:	For our church which helps us learn about God our Father
All:	we thank you, Lord Jesus.
Leader:	For your birth, Lord Jesus Christ,
	for your wonderful life,
	for your death on the cross for us,
	for your splendid resurrection,
	and for the sending of the Holy Spirit,
All:	we thank you, Lord Jesus. Amen.

(Amplified, Jersey, Milbrook St Matthew)

116 | | |
|---|---|
| *Minister:* | Let us thank the Lord for all his goodness. |
| *People:* | His mercy never fails. |
| *Minister:* | It is good to give thanks to God, |
| *People:* | and to remember all his blessings. |
| *Minister:* | We thank you, Lord, for all your works: |
| *Teenagers:* | for stars and sun, for light and life; |
| *Adults:* | for warmth and health and daily food, |
| *All:* | and all life's joys, we give you thanks. |
| *Minister:* | For all the blessings of our homes, |
| *Parents:* | the children you have blessed us with, |
| *Children:* | our parents' love and family life, |
| *All:* | and all our friends' and neighbours' help. |
| *Minister:* | For minds to learn, and books to read. |
| *Teenagers:* | For colleges and schools and all who teach. |
| *Adults:* | For jobs to do and leisure to spend. |
| *All:* | And all the colour and interest of life. |
| *Minister:* | For the gift of your word, the guide book of life. |
| *Choir:* | For the beauty of music, your praises to sing. |
| *Congregation:* | For our church and its people, we give you our thanks.   Amen. |

(St Ann's & St Aldhelm's, Radipole)

On Mothering Sunday

117 *Leader:* Let us thank God for mothers in all ages who have loved and served the Lord.

All: We thank you, Lord.

Leader: For Hannah who dedicated her son Samuel to your service, and for Eunice who taught her son Timothy the Holy Scriptures from his childhood.

All: We thank you, Lord.

Leader: For our mothers who have given us birth, and for their continued love and care for us.

All: We thank you, Lord.

Leader: And let us especially thank God for the example of obedience and humility of Mary, the mother of Jesus, her Saviour and ours.

All: We thank you, Lord, in Jesus' name.   Amen.

(*Family Worship, revised*)

A litany for the fruit of the Spirit

118 *Leader:* The harvest of the Spirit is love:
Lord Jesus, we know that you taught us to love one another, and yet we sometimes find ourselves hating other people. It is so hard to be loving when others annoy us or are nasty to us.
We need a spirit of love.

All: Please give us your Spirit, Lord Jesus.

Leader: The harvest of the Spirit is joy and peace:
Lord Jesus, there are some days when we wake up feeling miserable and out of sorts. We try to be calm but somehow we feel irritable and quarrelsome.
We need a spirit of joy and peace.

All: Please give us your Spirit, Lord Jesus.

Leader: The harvest of the Spirit is patience and kindness:
Lord Jesus, you know how impatient we can be with each other, especially when other people seem slow to understand us. Some days, instead of being kind, we

feel we really want to hurt people.

We need a spirit of patience and kindness.

All: Please give us your Spirit, Lord Jesus.

Leader: The harvest of the Spirit is goodness and faithfulness:
            Lord Jesus, sometimes we are in a mood when we want
            to be good and reliable. At other times we feel we just
            want to be bad. We cannot understand ourselves for
            being like this, but we are glad to know you understand
            us and still love us.

            We need a spirit of goodness and faithfulness.

All: Please give us your Spirit, Lord Jesus.

Leader: The harvest of the Spirit is gentleness and self-control:
            Lord Jesus, it is often lack of thought which causes us
            to be rough or even cruel. Strong feelings rise within
            us and we find it so hard to be in control of ourselves.

            We need a spirit of gentleness and self-control.

All: Please give us your Spirit, Lord Jesus.   Amen.

(Source not known)

A litany at Harvest Thanksgiving

119 *Leader:*   Lord, you have kept your gracious promise that while
                earth remains, seed-time and harvest shall not cease.

    All: We thank you, heavenly Father.

    Leader: For giving us the fruits of the earth in their seasons,
                to strengthen and make glad our hearts.

    All: We thank you, heavenly Father.

    Leader: For health and strength; for the sight of our eyes, for
                the hearing of our ears, the strength of our limbs, the
                power of our mind, and the energy which forges them
                into an instrument for your service.

    All: We thank you, heavenly Father.

    Leader: Lord, give us today our daily food so that we may have
                no anxiety about tomorrow, lest concern over money
                or family cares should blind our vision or distract our
                service for you:

    All: Give us today our daily bread.

Leader: By the exercise of hard work and thrift; by the co-operation of all sections of the community in working for the common good; and by the sympathy which provides for those in need at home and abroad:

All: Give us today our daily bread.

Leader: By seeking to relieve the millions of our fellow human beings who live in poverty, homelessness and hunger, and that we may bear each other's burdens according to your will:

All: Give us today our daily bread.

Leader: By daily feeding on your word, the Bible, by prayer and the reception of the Holy Communion of the body and blood of Christ, that we may evermore feed on him who is the true bread that comes down from heaven, Jesus Christ our Lord:

All: Give us today our daily bread.   Amen.

(Michael Botting, adapted from an unknown source)

120 *Leader:*   We give praise that once again God's ancient promise has been fulfilled and that seed-time and harvest have not ceased; and we give praise for all those who help to bring us our daily food: the farmers and fishermen, the transport and factory workers, the supermarket and shopkeepers.

All: We thank you, loving Father.

Leader: We know, however, that we do not live by food alone, but by every word of God. We therefore give praise for the Bible and for all those who have preserved it, translated it and printed it for us to read.

All: We thank you, loving Father.

Leader: We give praise for those who by their preaching and teaching sow the seed of your word in our hearts. And we give praise for your Holy Spirit who produces the fruit of love, joy and peace in our lives.

All: We thank you, loving Father.

Leader: But especially we give praise for your greatest gift to us of the Lord Jesus Christ, who is the Bread of Life;

and we give praise for his promise that whoever comes to him will not hunger and whoever believes on him will never thirst.

All: We thank you, loving Father, in his name.　Amen.

(Family Worship, revised)

A general litany of intercession

121 *Leader:* We can speak to God anywhere and at any time. But Jesus made this special promise to his followers: 'Where two or three have met together in my name, I am there among them.' Heavenly Father, we pray for our families and friends . . .

All: Yes, Lord, we thank you for the people who mean so much to us, and we do want you to bless them.

Leader: We pray for important people . . .

All: Yes, Lord, help them to be careful and courageous in what they do, carrying out your wishes.

Leader: We pray for our church, and for Christians everywhere . . .

All: Yes, Lord, help us together to serve you, and tell others of your love.

Leader: Today we pray for . . .

All: Yes, Lord, this is our special prayer, and we ask you to answer it, and all our prayers, in ways that will bring honour and respect to you.　Amen.

(Source unknown)

6

General Prayers

Prayers at the beginning of a service

122 *Minister:* Come close to God, and he will come
close to you.
The Lord our God is worthy to
receive glory and honour and power
for he has created and redeemed us.
Minister and people together: Heavenly Father, in our worship
help us to sing your praises,
confess our sins,
hear your word
and bring our prayers to you,
through Jesus Christ our
Lord. Amen.

(Family Worship)

123 *Minister:* As we come into God's house today, let us praise
him for his greatness and his love, and ask him for
his help and guidance in our daily lives.
Let us sit/kneel and say together:
All: Lord receive us with your blessing
Make us feel your presence now,
Help us as we come confessing,
With our heads, our hearts to bow.

Teach us by your word to know you,
Cause our lips true hymns to raise.
Show us all the debt we owe you,
Fill our hearts with love and praise.   Amen.

(Adapted from St Ann's & St Aldhelm's, Radipole)

Creation

124 Lord of the universe, we praise you for your creation; for the
wonder of space, the beauty of the world and the value of earth's
resources. Keep us from spoiling these gifts of yours by our
selfishness and help us to use them for the good of all people
and the glory of your name.   Amen.

(Family Worship)

125 Creator God, you have provided mankind with everything it
needs for life and health. Grant that the resources of the earth
may neither be hoarded by the selfish nor squandered by the
foolish, but that all may share your gifts; through our Lord Jesus
Christ.   Amen.

(Family Worship, revised)

Sunday

126 Almighty God, who has taught us to set apart the first day of
the week to remind us of the glorious resurrection of your Son,
teach us to use the gift of this day for the worship of our Lord,
and as means of refreshment for our souls and bodies; for Jesus
Christ's sake.   Amen.

(St Ann's & St Aldhelm's, Radipole)

127 O God our Father, we thank you for giving us Sunday to be a
day of rest, when we can be at home with those we love and
can go together to church.

Make Sunday a happy day for us all as we remember your
love and power in raising Jesus from the dead and giving us
your Holy Spirit, for Jesus Christ's sake.   Amen.

(Adapted from St Ann's & St Aldhelm's, Radipole)

Holidays and leisure

128 Heavenly Father, because you rested from your work of creation
we thank you for the opportunities we have of holidays and
leisure. Refresh our bodies, minds and souls, so that we may
return to our daily work better able to serve you, for Jesus'
sake. Amen.

(Family Worship)

Marriage

129 O God our Father, you made men and women to live together
in families. We pray that marriage may be held in honour, that
husbands and wives may live faithfully together, and that the
members of every family may grow in mutual understanding,
love and courtesy, through Jesus Christ our Lord. Amen.

(Family Worship)

God's will concerning marriage

130 Heavenly Father, we know that marriage is of your ordaining,
and that Jesus, your Son, blessed by his presence the wedding
at Cana in Galilee.
But we also learn from his example and teaching that marriage
is not your will for everyone.
Grant to each one of us the knowledge of your will, the grace
to accept it, and the power of your Spirit to obey it; for in your
will alone we find true peace and fulfilment. Amen.

(Michael Botting)

Homes and families

131 Dear God, we thank you for our homes and families,
for parents and brothers and sisters.
Help us to do our part to make our homes happy places,
by the way we behave in them
and by the words we speak in them.

May we be truthful and kind, helpful and unselfish.
Teach us to remember that you are our heavenly Father;
through Jesus Christ our Lord.   Amen.

(Source unknown)

Those with no parents

132 Heavenly Father, we pray for children who no longer have
mothers or fathers, and for those who have no proper homes.
We ask that you will especially help those who are looking after
them, that through their care these children may know you love
them very much. Through Jesus Christ your Son.   Amen.

(Family Worship, revised)

Industry and work

133 Almighty God, you give men and women wisdom to think and
skill to complete all kinds of work. Help those who labour with
hand and brain, that seeking the best in their job they may find
joy in their work; through Jesus Christ our Lord.   Amen.

(Family Worship)

134 O God, you have given all men and women their work to do.
Help them to do it with all their ability. Grant the spirit of
wisdom and justice to all leaders of industry and commerce.
Grant accuracy to those who work in offices and factories;
strengthen those who labour in the docks, on building sites or
in the fields; guard miners and others whose work is dangerous;
and help us all to follow in the steps of him who worked as a
carpenter, Jesus Christ our Lord.   Amen.

(Michael Botting)

The unemployed

135 Heavenly Father, creator and giver of all things,
your Son learned a carpenter's trade.
Protect and defend all who suffer poverty

and deprivation from being without work;
guide the people of this land
so to use its resources and wealth
that all may find employment
and receive just payment for their labour;
through Jesus Christ our Lord.   Amen.

(An Anglican Prayer Book, 1989
Church of the Province of Southern Africa, p. 88)

The Queen, her home and family and all who rule over us

136 Almighty God, our heavenly Father, we pray for our Queen,
that her home and the life of her family may always be based
on a Christian foundation and be an example to all her subjects.
Give wisdom to all who rule over us and help them to lead us
in ways of justice and peace; through Jesus Christ our
Lord.   Amen.

(Family Worship, revised)

Government

137 Almighty God, our heavenly Father, we pray for our Queen and
the Royal Family, the members of Parliament and all in
authority; that they may govern our country with wisdom and
understanding and for the good of your church and all people;
through Jesus Christ our Lord.   Amen.

(Family Worship)

138 Dear God, we thank you for the blessings of our country
and for the freedom which we enjoy.
We pray for our Queen and her family,
and for those who govern in her name.
Give them health and strength, wisdom and courage,
so that they may carry out their many duties
in the best interests of all our people.
Let all who have power remember they are your servants,
and that your Son came to serve rather than be served.
We ask this in his name, Jesus Christ, our Lord.   Amen.

(Anon, adapted)

139 Lord of heaven and earth, who gives life and breath to all and determines the boundaries of their habitation, we pray for our own nation that its affairs may be so ordered that peace and justice may prevail and Christian standards in public and private life may be maintained. Help us as your ambassadors so to live that our fellow countrymen may follow after you and find you; through Jesus Christ our Lord.   Amen.

(Source unknown)

Peace

140 We praise you, Lord, that you came to this world to bring peace on earth. We pray that the leaders of the nations and people everywhere may turn to you, the Prince of Peace, so that war and terror, cruelty and hatred may end, and peace and justice, kindness and love may reign. We ask this so that your will may be done on earth as it is in heaven, for your name's sake.   Amen.

(Family Worship, revised)

141 Dear Jesus, please help the people you have created to be at peace, have respect for each other and not be jealous of others. You have already given us freedom and taught us how to love one another. Please help us for your name's sake.   Amen.

(Laura Charlton, Bolton, aged 12)

The police

142 O God, whose will it is that men, women and children should live in an ordered society, we offer you our thanks for the general integrity of the police force.

Continue, we pray, to bless its members in their work of protecting persons and property. Give them good success in the detection of crime and the arrest of lawlessness. Save them from misuse of power and error of judgement. And so enable them to be instruments of your will and purpose. Through Jesus Christ our Lord.   Amen.

(Adapted from a prayer by Reginald Jackson that was published in a letter to the Church Times)

Road safety

143 Almighty God, giver of life and health, guide with your wisdom all who are striving to save from danger, injury and death, those who travel on our roads.

Grant to those who speed along our roads and motorways thought for others, and to those who walk on them or play by the side of them, thoughtful caution and care; through Jesus Christ our Lord. Amen.

(Adapted from a prayer published by RoSPA)

The local community

144 Lord of all grace and truth, who came to live among people in your own town of Nazareth, we pray that you will give us grace to live in our local community as salt to purify it, and as light to reveal your truth.

May we not be ashamed to acknowledge you as our Saviour; and may we learn so to love and honour all people, that peace and goodwill may prevail among us; for your name's sake. Amen.

(Michael Botting)

145 Lord Jesus Christ, you were born of a Jewish mother, but you took great delight in the faith both of a Syrian woman and a Roman soldier. You welcomed the Greeks, who were searching for you, and an African who carried your cross. Grant that we too may welcome people of every race as fellow-heirs in your kingdom. Amen.

(Adapted from a prayer of the Lutheran Church of Zululand)

Friends and neighbours

146 Heavenly Father, look in love on all our friends and neighbours. Keep them from all harm, deepen our friendship with them and may we all grow in the love of your Son, our Saviour and Friend, even Jesus Christ. Amen.

(Family Worship)

The family of the church

147 O God our Father, we praise you that through Jesus Christ your
     only Son you have adopted us into your family the church and
     made us your children. Help us to show our love and thanks
     to you by our care and concern for one another. Use us to spread
     your love to all the world in the power of your Holy Spirit, to
     the honour of your name.   Amen.

(Family Worship, revised)

148 Lord Jesus Christ, we ask you to bless the work of your church
     in this and every land, especially . . . So inspire each member
     by your Holy Spirit that we may be faithful witnesses by what
     we say and do. So may your kingdom be extended in people's
     hearts and lives.   Amen.

(St John's Church, Carlisle—adapted)

Our witness

149 O Lord God, we are all called to be your witnesses. Help us to
     make Jesus our Saviour known to others—through our words
     and our lives, through our prayers and our gifts; for his
     sake.   Amen.

(Family Worship)

Missionaries

150 Heavenly Father, we pray for those who have gone to other
     countries with the good news of Jesus. When their work is
     difficult and tiring, make them strong; when they are lonely
     and homesick, remind them that you are with them; when they
     are uncertain what to do, guide them. Keep them at all times
     loving you; for Jesus' sake.   Amen.

(Family Worship)

Christian service

151 Living Lord, we thank you for the honour and joy of being called to your service in the fellowship of your church.

Help us never to grow weary in well-doing; make us always ready to give a reason for the hope that is in us; and keep us faithful and vigilant as servants who wait for their Lord. We ask it for your name's sake.   Amen.

(Michael Botting)

Those in the pastoral ministry

152 Lord our God, you have chosen men and women to serve you in the ministry of your church and given them a perfect example in the person of your Son; pour your blessing on your servants today, especially those of our own church, that by word and deed they may proclaim your saving love, and so enable all your people to grow up into Christ, who is our Lord and head for ever and ever.   Amen.

(ACCM, adapted)

Those in training for pastoral ministry

153 Lord of the harvest, we pray for those training to become pastors and teachers in your church.
Give them a deepening assurance of your call,
an increasing experience of your life-giving Spirit,
a strong conviction of revealed truth
and a holy boldness to make it known;
that they may equip your people for work in your service and build up the body of Christ in faith and knowledge, to the glory of your great name.   Amen.

(Michael Botting)

The Bible

154 Heavenly Father, through the Bible you have shown the wonder
of your love for us in Jesus Christ. Help us to understand it
with our minds and apply it in our lives, for his sake.   Amen.

(Family Worship)

155 Almighty and everlasting God, who gave to your apostles grace
truly to believe and to preach your word, grant to your church
to love that word which they believed, and both to preach and
receive the same; through Jesus Christ our Lord.   Amen.

(Adapted—source unknown)

Church unity

156 Almighty Lord God, make us one with those whose lives are
dedicated to you; make us firm in the truth by the coming of
your Holy Spirit; show us the truth where we are ignorant; make
up for what we lack; make secure what we have, and gather us
all together in the heavenly kingdom in Jesus Christ our
Lord.   Amen.

(Apostolic Constitutions)

The church crèche

157 We thank you, Lord Jesus, that you showed your love for little
children when you blessed those brought to you by their parents.
We ask your blessing on the children in our crèche today during
this hour of worship.

May the Christian love of the helpers show these little ones
something of your love, and contribute to their spiritual
upbringing in the family of the church; for your name's
sake.   Amen.

(Michael Botting)

Children

158 Dear heavenly Father, we thank you for the children you have committed to our care in this church. Make us aware of their needs and ready to listen to them, as well as talk to them. Grant especial grace and wisdom to those who teach them, that they may grow up to know, love and serve you, for Jesus' sake.   Amen.

(Michael Botting)

School

159 Lord Jesus Christ, the source of all knowledge and truth, give to all who teach the spirit of wisdom and understanding, and grant that all who learn may have a true judgement in all things, that we might be an upright and God-fearing people, for your sake.   Amen.

(Family Worship)

160 Lord Jesus, the Bible tells us that even at the young age of twelve you were looking for answers to your many questions about life, among the clever teachers in Jerusalem. Give us all a thirst after the truth, about ourselves, our country, our world and about yourself. Help our parents, and our teachers at church and school, to be able to answer our questions in words that make sense to us, that we may grow in wisdom and stature as you did; for your name's sake.   Amen.

(Michael Botting)

Children at play

161 Lord Jesus Christ, we know that you loved to have children around you, taking an interest in their games. Help all of us who have the care of children, to guide them in ways that are noble, right, pure and true, that they might find fulfilment and happiness in this life, and afterwards enter into your heavenly joy; for your name's sake.   Amen.

(Michael Botting)

Young people

162 We pray, our Father, for the teenagers of our church.

Help us who are older to remember the adventure and joy of youth as well as the temptation and frustrations; and enable us to assist our young people by our prayers, our example, and our friendship.

Help those in their teens to respond to the love of Jesus, to yield to him their allegiance, and to serve him as Lord and Saviour all their days; for his name's sake.   Amen.

(Michael Botting)

Youth leaders

163 We thank you, heavenly Father, for all who serve young people in the youth organisations and Bible classes of our church. Keep them fresh week by week and help us all to come to know and serve your Son Jesus Christ, our Lord.   Amen.

(St John's Church, Carlisle—adapted)

A church youth club/centre

164 We pray, heavenly Father, for the work of our youth club/centre. Grant compassion and zeal to the leaders and helpers that they may be sensitive to the real needs of club members, especially those from disturbed and unstable backgrounds.

Give divine wisdom to the management committee, especially in appointing staff, dealing with day-to-day problems and raising funds.

Particularly, we pray that the club/centre may become a place where young people not only enjoy themselves in a positive way, but also discover for themselves new life in Jesus Christ. We ask this in Jesus' name.   Amen.

(Michael Botting)

Young mothers' group

165 We praise you, Lord Jesus, that through your holy birth at Bethlehem you raised the status of motherhood.

We bring before you everything that being a mother means to us. We offer you all our joys and frustrations, our ambitions and disappointments, our hopes and our fears. Thank you that you understand and care about them all. Amen.

(Michael Botting)

Men's group

166 Strong Son of God, our Saviour, who chose for your first followers not the great or exalted but ordinary men from the common ways of life, and gave them each a place in your service: we thank you for calling us to serve you in the fellowship of the church in this our day.

Keep us faithful to our calling; strengthen the bonds of brotherhood that unite us to each other; and show us how best we may bear witness as Christian men in our homes, our places of work, and in the life of our community, to the honour and praise of your name. Amen.

(Frank Colquhoun)

Those facing retirement

167 Heavenly Father, you have ordained that mankind should both work and rest. We pray for those whose working life is drawing to a close and who are now facing retirement.

Prepare them in mind and spirit for this change in their life's pattern, that their future days and years may be positive and creative, beneficial to the work of the church, and rewarding to all who know them; for Jesus Christ's sake. Amen.

(Michael Botting)

Stewardship

168 Lord Jesus Christ, you have taught us that we cannot love God and money, and that all our possessions are a trust from you. Teach us to be faithful stewards of our time, our talents, and our money, that we may help others and extend your kingdom; for your name's sake.   Amen.

(Family Worship)

Offering prayers

169 As you have given us, may we give
our money, work and care.
As you have loved us, may we love,
all people everywhere.   Amen.

(Eveline Wyatt and Brian Ogden)

170 Lord, we have given our money, and it is especially for the work of your church. But it is not the only thing we need to give you: our life, our strength, our abilities all need to be brought to you—all need to be under your control—and that is what we want them to be. So please accept both our money and ourselves, for Jesus Christ's sake.   Amen.

(Anon)

Grace at a church lunch

171 Lord Jesus, we remember how you brought blessing to many meal-times when on earth:
    sharing a wedding feast,
    feeding the five thousand,
    having breakfast by the seaside.
Bless our food and fellowship today.
May this be a time when we experience your risen presence,
and get to know some people better,
and others for the first time;
for your name's sake.   Amen.

(Michael Botting)

Those in need

172 O God of love, whose compassion does not fail, we bring to
you the sufferings of all humankind: the despair of the homeless;
the sighing of prisoners, especially of those held unjustly; the
pains of the sick and injured; the sorrows of the bereaved; the
helplessness of the aged and frail. In your great mercy comfort
and relieve them, our Father, according to their various needs;
for the sake of your Son and our Saviour Jesus Christ.   Amen.

(Michael Botting, adapted from an anonymous prayer)

173 Lord God, we ask you to give us your blessing:
to your church—holiness,
to the world—peace,
to this nation—justice,
and to all people—knowledge of your law.
Keep safe our families, protect the weak, heal the sick, comfort
the dying and bring us all to a joyful resurrection.
We ask these things through Jesus Christ our Lord.   Amen.

(An Anglican Prayer Book, 1989
Church of the Province of Southern Africa, p. 50)

The homeless and hungry

174 Have mercy, O Lord our God, on those who have been robbed
of homes and families by war, oppression or famine, and today
we especially think of the people of . . . Guide us and all people
as we seek to show them the love of Christ by our prayerful
concern and practical action; for his sake.   Amen.

(Family Worship)

175 Dear God, help us to share out all the good things in this world.
Many people do not have any money and can't buy food to eat
and get medical treatment. These people don't have any fresh
water and have to wash and drink from dirty rivers. Please help
us to help them.   Amen.

(Lucy Sutton, Leicester, aged 10)

The sick and suffering

176 O God, the source of life and health, we pray for those who are
ill, especially . . . Give doctors and nurses skill to make them
well again, and grant that during their illness they may learn
more of your love and care; through Jesus Christ.   Amen.

(Family Worship)

Hospital staff

177 Heavenly Father, we pray for nurses, doctors, surgeons and all
who work in hospitals. We pray that your love, care and healing
power may flow through their eyes, their lips and their hands,
bringing health, new life, comfort and peace; through Jesus
Christ our Lord.   Amen.

(Michael Botting)

178 Heavenly Father, we thank you for the laws of health which
you have built into our bodies to help doctors and nurses in
their fight against sickness. Help them to realise how much
they depend on your blessing, and continue to reveal more and
more cures for illness; through Jesus Christ our Lord.   Amen.

(St John's Church, Carlisle—adapted)

179 Almighty and everlasting God, whose Son was the healer of the
sick, we ask you to heal and comfort those who may be lonely
or disabled, and not as fortunate as ourselves. Help us to care
for the elderly and think about the blind and deaf; through Jesus
Christ our Lord.   Amen.

(Jim Fisher, Bolton, aged 12)

180 Heavenly Father, help all the people who are sick. Comfort
them with your presence from day to day. Help those who suffer
from starvation or homelessness. Be with those in hospital who
suffer mentally and physically. Be with those who care for the
sick, especially the nurses and doctors, every day of their working
lives. We ask this in your name.   Amen.

(Claire Latchford, Bolton, aged 12)

181 Father Almighty, whose Son Jesus Christ healed the sick, help all
the people in this world who are blind, deaf, dumb, elderly,
housebound, lonely and disabled. Help their friends to cope with
everyday life and with the disability. We ask this of you. Amen.

(Claire Latchford, Bolton, aged 12)

On recovery from illness

182 O Lord our healer, whose will for your children is wholeness
and healing, we praise you for the measure of renewed health
you have granted to your servant(s) . . .
Continue your gracious work in his/her life; and bring to fullness
of life in heaven hereafter; for Jesus Christ's sake. Amen.

(Michael Botting)

The bereaved

183 O God our Father, we pray for those whose life is saddened by
the death of a relative or friend, especially . . . Be with them
in their loneliness and give them faith to look beyond their
present trouble to Jesus, the one who died and rose again, and
who lives for evermore. Amen.

(Family Worship)

The bereaved and all who suffer as the result of war

184 Father, we remember how your Son, during the time of his
ministry on earth, had great compassion for those who suffered.
We bring to you those who still suffer as a result of war. Hear
our prayer, Father, for those who live with pain and scars of
bodily injury; for those whose minds are shattered by the horrors
which they witnessed or endured; for those who have been
bereaved; for those who do not believe in you or trust their
fellow human beings.
Grant to them peace of mind and heart, and relief from all their
suffering, through Jesus Christ our Lord. Amen.

(Adapted from a prayer published by the Church Society)

Remembrance

185 Almighty and eternal God, we remember before you all those
who have laid down their lives in the service of their country
in wartime, and we offer you our humble thanks for their example
of courage and devotion to duty.

  Help us to realise that apart from you we cannot know true
peace. Turn us again to yourself, Lord, that we may enjoy once
more the blessings which you have promised to all who love
and honour your holy name; through Jesus Christ our
Lord.   Amen.

(Adapted from a prayer published by the Church Society)

Heaven

186 Bring us, Lord, at our last awakening into the house and gate
of heaven, to enter into that gate and dwell in that house, where
there shall be no darkness nor dazzling, but one equal light; no
noise nor silence, but one equal music; no fears nor hopes, but
one equal possession; no ends nor beginnings, but one equal
eternity; in the dwelling-place of your majesty and glory, world
without end.   Amen.

(John Donne, slightly adapted)

A prayer of commitment

187 Teach us, good Lord, to serve you as you deserve, to give and
not to count the cost, to fight and not to heed the wounds, to
toil and not to seek for rest, to labour and not to ask for any
reward, except that of knowing that we do your will; through
Jesus Christ our Lord.   Amen

(After St Ignatius Loyola)

Living dangerously

188 O God, whose love and power are shown in giving us eternal
life, we ask for strength of faith sufficient to dare the hazards

of living; so that although we do not see you, we endure as
though we did.

Through your Son, who by taking flesh committed himself
to the uncertainties of human life; Jesus Christ our
Lord.   Amen.

(Michael Botting, adapted from an anonymous prayer)

Obedience

189 Stop us, God, from trying to make you what we want you to be,
instead of obeying you.
Stop us putting the idols of our own pride and fear
where you ought to be.
Give us the insight to worship you as the real, living God, and
to offer ourselves as living sacrifices truly pleasing to you. Change
our minds and our behaviour to suit your purpose for us, so
that we may discover your will and do what you want.   Amen.

(From New Prayers for Worship by Alan Gaunt)

An updated 'Prayer of St Francis'

190 Where there is extravagance and luxury,
     let me sow the love of simplicity.
Where there is greed and the desire always to have more,
     let me sow contentment.
Where there is envy of what others are getting,
     let me sow humility.
Where there is indifference to the sufferings of others,
     let me sow compassion.   Amen.

(John R.H. Moorman)

(There is no evidence that the prayer, commonly attributed to St Francis, was written
by him, seeing that the first known appearance of the prayer was in a French periodical
in January 1913, seven hundred years after Francis died. The above was a suggestion
of what sort of prayer Francis might have written today. It was included in a letter
to the *Church Times* of 15th June 1979 from Bishop Moorman, now deceased, who
was an acknowledged world authority on the saint.)

The prayer of St Richard of Chichester

191   Thanks be to thee, O Lord Jesus Christ, for all the pains and insults which thou has borne for us. O merciful Redeemer, Friend and Brother, may we know thee more clearly, love thee more dearly, and follow thee more nearly, now and for evermore.   Amen.

Before leaving public worship

192   Be with us, Lord, as we go out into the world. May the lips that have sung your praises always speak the truth; may the ears which have heard your word listen only to what is good and may our lives as well as our worship be always pleasing in your sight, for the glory of Jesus Christ our Lord.   Amen.

(Family Worship)

193   Be with us, Lord, as we leave your house, and grant that the prayers which we have said and the words which we have heard may help us in our daily lives. May we never forget that you are always near us, and may we be given grace to do all things to your glory; through Jesus Christ our Lord.   Amen.

(Adapted from Christ Church, Flackwell Heath Family Service)

194   Please, Lord, lead us into this coming week. Help us to believe that you are close by us; keep us from making mistakes and help us never to disappoint you.

    When we face hard decisions or difficult work, when we enjoy ourselves and have fun with others, may we know that you share these times with us, and may we be ready to tell others about you, and about your Son, Jesus Christ, our Saviour, in whose name we pray.   Amen.

(Anon, adapted)

7

Visual Prayers

I mention in the Guidelines for those leading Family Services, at the beginning of this Section, that there is a danger during the intercessions of what has been described as 'shuffling boredom'. I had, of course, got the children especially in mind, but I suspect that if we are honest this part of the service can be a time when we are all tempted to switch off. Whether we are having to cope with children or not, we make it easier for ourselves to succumb by sitting comfortably and closing our eyes. I well remember the South American preacher and pastor, Juan Carlos Ortiz, saying to me that he encouraged his congregation to keep their eyes open during their time of intercession. 'After all,' he explained, 'if they are praising God for the wonder of creation, how much better if they can see it around them. When praying for one another, especially when saying the Grace, why not actually look at each other?'

So how can we help prevent our minds wandering during this part of the Family Service? The answer may somewhat depend on the extent to which you can easily darken your church building during your church service. If the church is easily blacked-out, or a daylight screen and back-projector can be quickly installed, try showing some slides during the intercession. For example, when interceding for missionaries, whether from your church or not, project some coloured slides onto a screen showing the missionaries themselves, the area where they live, and the work in which they are involved. It is obviously important not to have too many slides or it will develop into a slide show rather than a time of intercession.

Another approach that can be easily accomplished in daylight is the use of the overhead projector (OHP) and acetates. These can be used in more than one way. For example, your church will be regularly praying for the sick, so have an acetate with some illustrations round the sides of the sick-room or hospital. This can be done with permanent ink pens. Then using washable ink pens add the names of the sick requiring prayer at that particular time. These can be brought up to date when next praying for the sick.

Another permanent ink acetate could be for the Church Council Meeting, perhaps having an agenda background. The main items for the next meeting can be added in washable ink. Other such acetates could be for missionaries (if the above method is impractical), for the homeless and hungry, for war-stricken areas and for our leaders, for whom the Apostle Paul especially exhorted us to pray (1 Timothy 2:1–4). In the last case an acetate could have the Houses of Parliament at the bottom with Big Ben partly rising on the right-hand edge. The latest national crises can be written in with washable ink.

There will be occasions, however, when matters for prayer occur that deserve special acetates, even though they are unlikely to be used again. Such an event recently occurred for me when I was using visual prayers, namely the release of John McCarthy, the former hostage, and the anticipation of the release of Terry Waite. I had an acetate showing both their pictures.

How do we make our acetates? Ideally, we use the artistic talent that is already available in our congregation. If this is the case it is important that we provide adequate notice of what we require and also pay out-of-pocket expenses from church funds. If such talent is not available, then the permanent ink acetates could be prepared professionally and would be a once-off expense. It should not be too difficult for the additional non-permanent part to be added legibly.

Another valuable asset is the photocopier, especially if it can enlarge and reduce. Nowadays it is possible to buy special acetates that can be used in a copier, but on no account use the wrong kind! With the aid of the copier and the correct acetates you can copy photographs, magazine and newspaper pictures, and in the size you want them. Though they will be black and white, a little colour can be added with OHP coloured pens. You can find further information on the use of OHPs and the making of acetates in my books on talks for Family Services: *For All the Family*, *More For All the Family* and the recently revised edition of *Teaching the Families*, all published by Kingsway. The last-named book also gives full details of how to make and use a daylight screen with back-projection.

It is important that the person leading the intercessions does not operate the slide projector or OHP, but has an assistant. The latter will either need a full script of the prayers or have a very clear signal from the prayer leader, so that the visuals do appear at the exact moment required.

Finally, I would suggest that when using this method of praying in church you point out that no one is obliged to look at the visuals, because some people may be able to concentrate, and therefore pray better, without them. I am not aware that any research has been attempted to discover how effective this visual method of praying is. One thing I do know is that eye-gate is far more effective than ear-gate alone.

Section 2

FAMILY PRAYERS AT HOME

I

Introduction

Before beginning this Section I visited the three Christian bookshops in Chester, which between them covered a wide spectrum of Christian spirituality, and I enquired about the demand from the Christian public for assistance with material for family prayers. The response in every case was almost the same: practically no demand at all. However, one shop drew my attention to a book, *Prayers for Families*, edited by Peter Toon and published by Hodder & Stoughton in 1990. This book is an updated and abridged edition of prayers collected by Benjamin Jenks (1646–1724), Rector of Harley in Shropshire, and originally published for the benefit of families in his congregation. Dr Toon was not the first to be impressed by Jenks' collection. Charles Simeon (1759–1836), Fellow of King's College, and Vicar of Holy Trinity, Cambridge, for over fifty years, discovered them. He revised them to take account of the emerging industrial society, and published them in 1808. There were at least thirteen editions in the next fifty years.

What then is the place for family prayers at home today? I strongly suspect that the reason for lack of demand for help is not that parents feel adequately equipped for the task, but rather that the sheer pressure of modern computerised life has squeezed the activity out of Christian family thinking. I noted that Dr Toon dedicated his book to five people, whom he names and describes as 'a family which prays'. However, I would be interested to know for how long Jenks' prayers are used. Excellent though they are, steeped in biblical quotation and allusion, they are all much too long for use in today's normal household, especially if there are children and teenagers present. Also, there seems to be an extended emphasis on sin and the need for repentance that almost exceeds that of the *Book of Common Prayer*.

In the very first paragraph of the introduction to this book I mentioned that my wife and I began prayers with our children over their cots, so there was never a time in their lives when they were not aware that we prayed. As our children developed from babyhood they shared with us on weekdays Bible reading and prayer around the breakfast table, using schemes suggested by organisations such as the Bible Reading Fellowship and Scripture Union. Because we were concerned that this time should be a shared experience, we usually expected everyone to take turns in the actual reading of the Bible. However, we gradually became aware that this family prayer time was tending to become a somewhat painful exercise in testing our children's reading ability, rather than a happy devotional meeting with our heavenly Father.

Also, there were further problems relating to school and work, coupled with the genuine desire that our children should increasingly feel free to make their own choices about life, not only in mundane matters such as the clothes they wore or the decor of their bedrooms, but also in the far more important matter of how they conducted their own spiritual affairs. We consciously stopped family prayers as such, but twenty years later our children, their spouses and our four grandchildren are active members of their own parish churches. So our action does not seem to have irreparably damaged their spiritual progress. I still believe there is a place for family prayers at home with our children, at least in their younger years, though with hindsight we might have ordered ours differently.

In the chapter that follows I have selected Bible readings from books that seem especially relevant to families. None of them is very long, in the hope that family prayers are more likely to continue if they don't become wearisome. Twelve readings are listed for each day, so that one can be used for each month of the year. The two prayers provided for each day take up some, but not all, of the themes of the readings, based on the New International Version. These are all written by me, so none is acknowledged. The effect of this plan should be that although the same prayers are used each month, they will have a different significance because the Bible readings will not have been the same.

Where Christian festivals come on a fixed day in the year, the readings reflect this (e.g. Epiphany on 6th January). Other festivals will have to be supplemented from Chapter 3. Other general prayers from Chapter 4 can be fitted in as appropriate.

In quite a number of places the prayers assume that family prayer takes place in the morning, probably at the breakfast table. If this is not so in your situation, then very slight adjustments will have to be made.

2

A Monthly Cycle of Prayer

Day 1

Jan	Genesis 1:1–5	*May*	Proverbs 1:1–7	*Sep*	Psalm 73:1–14
Feb	Luke 1:1–10	*Jun*	Romans 1:16–20	*Oct*	Acts 1:1–8
Mar	Luke 18:1–8	*Jul*	Genesis 28:1–5	*Nov*	1 Timothy 1:12–19
Apr	Psalm 1	*Aug*	Luke 8:1–8	*Dec*	Exodus 1:1–14

195 O God, Creator of the universe, we thank you for the knowledge that you have the whole world in your hand, yet you are concerned for the daily events of our homes and our lives, and you even long to hear our prayers.

We ask that you will daily speak to each of us as we read the Bible together, that we may be obedient to what we hear, and each of our lives may prosper, to the glory of your name.   Amen.

196 O God, it is all of your loving grace and goodness, seen especially on the cross of Jesus, that we can come before you and call you our Father. May we never be ashamed to admit that we follow you. Help us to shine for you in our small corner of the world today, for Jesus' sake.   Amen.

Day 2

Jan	Genesis 1:26–28	*Mar*	Luke 18:9–14	*May*	Proverbs 1:8–19
Feb	Luke 1:11–25	*Apr*	Psalm 2	*Jun*	Romans 3:19–26

Jul	Genesis 28:10–17	*Sep*	Psalm 73:15–28	*Nov*	1 Timothy 2:1–8
Aug	Luke 8:9–15	*Oct*	Acts 1:9–14	*Dec*	Exodus 1:15–22

197 Our Almighty Creator and Redeemer, your ways are often very strange and beyond our understanding. However, we know you love to hear the prayers of those who are humble. We pray today especially for those in authority: for our Queen and the Royal Family, for the Members of Parliament and those in the armed services, for our (Lord) Mayor, local councillors, the police and magistrates. Grant them special wisdom in all they do that we may live peaceful and quiet lives in godliness and holiness. We ask this in the all powerful name of our ascended Lord Jesus Christ.   Amen.

198 We stand amazed that the Lord Jesus shed his blood on the cross, so that we who put our trust in him are freely saved from our sins. We are seen by you, O God, as perfect and blameless. We each thank you for being our wonderful Saviour, and pray that we may live for his glory wherever we are today, for his sake.   Amen.

Day 3

Jan	Genesis 1:29–2:3	*May*	Proverbs 1:20–31	*Sep*	Psalm 78:1–8
Feb	Luke 1:26–38	*Jun*	Romans 5:1–8	*Oct*	Acts 2:1–13
Mar	Luke 18:18–30	*Jul*	Genesis 29:1–14	*Nov*	1 Timothy 6:11–21
Apr	Psalm 8	*Aug*	Luke 8:16–21	*Dec*	Exodus 2:1–10

199 We have so many things to thank you for, O God our Father, but especially today we thank you that it was part of your loving purpose that children should be brought up in happy families. We pray that we may all learn from one another. We ask, too, that you will help us to keep one day a week especially as a family day for worship, rest and leisure; for your sake and ours, in Jesus' name.   Amen.

200 We thank you, our heavenly Father, that we do not have to live the Christian life on our own, but you have given us your powerful Holy Spirit to help us fight the good fight of faith and take hold of eternal life. May his flame burn brightly in our lives today, for Jesus' sake.   Amen.

Day 4

Jan	Genesis 2:15–24	*May*	Proverbs 2:1–11	*Sep*	Psalm 84
Feb	Luke 1:39–56	*Jun*	Romans 8:28–32	*Oct*	Acts 2:14–21
Mar	Luke 18:18–30	*Jul*	Genesis 29:15–20	*Nov*	2 Timothy 3:10–17
Apr	Psalm 13	*Aug*	Luke 8:22–25	*Dec*	Exodus 2:11–17

201 We thank you, O God our Father, for some wonderful examples of love in the Bible: for Adam's love at first sight for Eve, for Jacob's patient love for Rachel, and for the loving teaching from the Scriptures given to young Timothy by his mother and grandmother from infancy.

Deepen the love in our family for each other and for all who live around us, for Jesus' sake.   Amen.

202 Deepen our faith, O Lord, that we may trust you, even though the days ahead sometimes seem dark and uncertain. Help us to hold on to the truth that in all things you work for the good of those who love you, who have been called according to your purposes.   Amen.

Day 5

Jan	Genesis 3:1–7	*May*	Proverbs 3:1–6	*Sep*	Psalm 85
Feb	Luke 1:57–66	*Jun*	Romans 8:33–39	*Oct*	Acts 2:22–28
Mar	Luke 18:31–43	*Jul*	Genesis 30:22–28	*Nov*	Philemon 1–11
Apr	Psalm 15	*Aug*	Luke 8:26–33	*Dec*	Exodus 2:18–25

203 We confess before you, O holy God, that we so easily fall into temptation, and then into sin. We know that you can only receive into heaven those who are blameless. We therefore thank you that in your great love for us you have made a way to restore us to yourself. Help us to live today as those who know they are under your smile.   Amen.

204 We thank you for all the joy that comes to a home when a baby is born. We pray for those we know who are expecting new babies soon. We pray about all the special plans that have to be made. Bring to our minds any ways in which we, as a family, could offer help. May each family know that nothing can separate them from your love, as it is seen in the Lord Jesus. We ask this in his name.   Amen.

Day 6

Jan	Matthew 2:1–12	*May*	Proverbs 3:7–12	*Sep*	Psalm 90:1–12
Feb	Luke 1:67–80	*Jun*	Romans 12:1–8	*Oct*	Acts 2:29–36
Mar	Luke 19:1–10	*Jul*	Genesis 35:9–15	*Nov*	Philemon 12–25
Apr	Psalm 16	*Aug*	Luke 8:34–39	*Dec*	Exodus 3:1–10

205 We thank you, heavenly Father, for the wonderful way in which you have made yourself known to people in the world: to men like Jacob and Moses, Zechariah and Zacchaeus, and very specially to the wise men, who were led by a star to the baby Jesus. Guide us as we travel to the heavenly city that we, and everyone, may know Jesus as the true and living way; for his name's sake.   Amen.

206 As the wise men of old were very generous in the wonderful gifts they brought for the Lord Jesus, help us, dear Lord, to be generous in our giving and our hospitality, remembering both the needs of the church and the poor; for your name's sake.   Amen.

Day 7

Jan	Genesis 3:8–15	*May*	Proverbs 3:27–35	*Sep*	Psalm 91
Feb	Luke 2:1–7	*Jun*	Romans 12:14–21	*Oct*	Acts 2:37–41
Mar	Luke 19:28–44	*Jul*	Genesis 37:1–11	*Nov*	Hebrews 11:1–6
Apr	Psalm 19	*Aug*	Luke 8:40–48	*Dec*	Exodus 11:1–10

207 We praise you today, almighty Father, as we see your loving hand at work in the world, partly through the wonderful design of creation, but very especially through the birth, life, death, resurrection and exaltation of Jesus as Lord and Christ. Give us grace to come to him in sorrow for our sins, and faith to accept him as our Saviour and King; for his sake and ours. Amen.

208 We confess, O God, how easily we can be jealous of other people, whatever age we might be, because they have things we want. Help us not to forget the teaching of the Bible that we should aim to live at peace with everyone, never allow ourselves to be overcome by evil, but overcome evil with good, remembering that the Lord Jesus prayed for those who crucified him. Amen.

Day 8

Jan	Genesis 3:17–24	*May*	Proverbs 4:1–9	*Sep*	Psalm 93
Feb	Luke 2:8–20	*Jun*	1 Corinthians 2:1–5	*Oct*	Acts 2:42–47
Mar	Luke 19:45–48	*Jul*	Genesis 37:12–24	*Nov*	Hebrews 11:8–12
Apr	Psalm 22:1–18	*Aug*	Luke 8:49–56	*Dec*	Exodus 12:1–11

209 We rejoice, heavenly King, that you are our God and you reign in this world. Give us the faith to believe that as we make our journey through life, we, like Abraham, are travelling to that heavenly city, of which you are the architect and builder. We pray in Jesus' name. Amen.

210 Help us to understand, loving Father, that sometimes we have to suffer for following you, just as the Lord Jesus had to suffer on the cross before he could bring us salvation. We pray today for any who are especially suffering for their faith, that they may be strong through the power of your Holy Spirit. Amen.

Day 9

Jan	Genesis 4:1–7	*May*	Proverbs 4:10–19	*Sep*	Psalm 95
Feb	Luke 2:21–32	*Jun*	1 Corinthians 12:12–20	*Oct*	Acts 3:1–10
Mar	Luke 20:1–8			*Nov*	Hebrews 11:17–22
Apr	Psalm 22:19–31	*Jul*	Genesis 37:25–36	*Dec*	Exodus 12:12–20
		Aug	Luke 9:10–17		

211 In our hearts we sing to you, Sovereign Lord, because you are our Maker and Saviour. By sending to us your only Son, the Lord Jesus, you have made possible a way of escape from the terrible results of sin. Through the work of your church may many have eyes to see your salvation and become part of Christ's body. We ask it in his name. Amen.

212 Like the Apostles, Peter and John, we may not have much to offer you, O Lord, but like Abel we can bring you our best, and like the little boy in the Gospels, we can bring all we have for you to bless. May your love for us inspire us to give generously of our salary and our pocket-money for the good of those in need. For your name's sake. Amen.

Day 10

Jan	Genesis 4:8–16	*May*	Proverbs 4:20–27	*Sep*	Psalm 100
Feb	Luke 2:33–40	*Jun*	1 Corinthians 13	*Oct*	Acts 3:11–16
Mar	Luke 20:9–19	*Jul*	Genesis 39:1–10	*Nov*	Hebrews 12:1–6
Apr	Psalm 23	*Aug*	Luke 9:18–27	*Dec*	Exodus 12:21–30

213 Shepherd King, we come to praise and thank you for all your goodness to us and your guidance. In our day-to-day walk with you may we at all times avoid evil and fix our eyes on Jesus, the author and perfector of our faith, who for the joy set before him endured the cross, scorning its shame, and is now seated at the right hand of your throne. Amen.

214 All-loving Lord, we know that love is the supreme gift and fruit of the Spirit. We confess to you that we are so often neither patient nor kind, but envious, boastful and proud. Help us to realise, unlike Cain, that we are our brother's keeper. So grant us an increase in love for you and for all those around us, and very specially for those in need. For your loving name's sake. Amen.

Day 11

Jan	Genesis 6:9–22	*May*	Proverbs 6:6–11	*Sep*	Psalm 103:1–12
Feb	Luke 2:41–52	*Jun*	1 Corinthians	*Oct*	Acts 4:23–31
Mar	Luke 20:20–26		15:1–11	*Nov*	Hebrews 12:7–13
Apr	Psalm 24	*Jul*	Genesis 39:11–23	*Dec*	Exodus 12:31–42
		Aug	Luke 9:28–36		

215 We thank you, heavenly Father, for the wonderful life and
example of the Lord Jesus: his thirst for knowledge as a child,
his fearless teaching as a man, his revelation to his disciples on
the mountain of his divinity, supremely confirmed by his
glorious resurrection from the dead and ascension into heaven.
May we never rest content until our lives reflect his
glory.   Amen.

216 Help us to grasp, loving Father, that we may have to suffer in
this world, sometimes because you are needing to show us
something wrong in our lives. You are treating us kindly as
your children. But sometimes we may have to suffer innocently,
like Joseph of old, because he stood up for what was right. We
pray today for all who are in prison, like him, because they have
done the same. May they know that you have not forgotten
them, that in your time you will redeem their lives from the
pit and crown them with love and compassion.   Amen.

Day 12

Jan	Genesis 7:13–24	*May*	Proverbs 6:12–19	*Sep*	Psalm 103:13–22
Feb	Luke 3:15–22	*Jun*	1 Corinthians	*Oct*	Acts 5:1–11
Mar	Luke 21:1–15		15:12–19	*Nov*	James 2:14–24
Apr	Psalm 27:1–6	*Jul*	Genesis 40:1–15	*Dec*	Exodus 20:1–7
		Aug	Luke 9:37–45		

217 We know, almighty Father, that when we leave our home today,
to go out into the world to work, shop, learn or play, there will
be other gods that want our worship. One of the biggest
temptations will be to love money, which is the root of all evil.
Another temptation will be to go with the crowd and use your

name as a swearword. Guard us, Lord, from these things, for your name's sake.   Amen.

218 We confess, heavenly Father, that our faith can so easily be in words only, whereas those who want our help need action. So help us think of ways in which we can show our genuine faith in you by our practical aid for our needy neighbours, for their sakes and yours.   Amen.

Day 13

Jan	Genesis 8:15–22	*May*	Proverbs 8:1–11	*Sep*	Psalm 111
Feb	Luke 4:1–13	*Jun*	1 Corinthians	*Oct*	Acts 5:12–16
Mar	Luke 22:1–12		15:20–26	*Nov*	James 3:1–12
Apr	Psalm 27:7–14	*Jul*	Genesis 40:16–23	*Dec*	Exodus 20:8–17
		Aug	Luke 9:57–62		

219 We know, almighty God, that though the Lord Jesus was tempted, he never sinned. Strengthen us as we face our temptations today: the temptations to disobey your commandments, to misuse our tongue and to find excuses for not following you sincerely. Grant us the will to renounce the devil as Jesus did, for your glory.   Amen.

220 We thank you, heavenly Father, for the wonderful signs of your presence in the world: for the regular sequence of the seasons of the year, reminding us that you will never again curse the earth; the wonderful repetition of the Lord Jesus' Supper, reminding us of his death for us, and that he has been raised to life. Finally, we thank you for the many changed lives brought about by the preaching of the gospel, beginning with the apostles. Grant that our lives may be a further sign and witness that you reign.   Amen.

Day 14

Jan	Genesis 11:1–9	*Mar*	Luke 22:13–23	*May*	Proverbs 8:12–21
Feb	Luke 4:14–21	*Apr*	Psalm 29	*Jun*	1 Corinthians
					15:50–58

Jul Genesis 41:1–14	*Sep* Psalm 112	*Nov* James 4:4–10
Aug Luke 10:25–37	*Oct* Acts 5:17–26	*Dec* Isaiah 11:1–9

221 Grant us, almighty God, a proper fear of your name, that we
may ascribe to you glory, humbly submit our lives to you, resist
the devil and hate evil. So may we all discover your special
strength in our lives and that you bless us with your
peace.   Amen.

222 We thank you, heavenly Father, that part of the special message
of the Lord Jesus was to proclaim freedom to prisoners and
release for the oppressed. We rejoice at how Joseph and the
apostles were eventually freed from their captivity. Help us to
take to heart the message of the Lord's great parable of the Good
Samaritan and seek to bring comfort to all those in need who
come our way; for your name's sake.   Amen.

Day 15

Jan Genesis 12:1–7	*May* Proverbs 9:10–18	*Sep* Psalm 113
Feb Luke 4:22–30	*Jun* 2 Corinthians	*Oct* Acts 5:27–32
Mar Luke 22:24–30	5:16–6:2	*Nov* James 5:13–20
Apr Psalm 30	*Jul* Genesis 41:15–24	*Dec* Isaiah 35
	Aug Luke 10:38–42	

223 We know only too well, O Lord, that sometimes we feel
miserable for no apparent reason. So we thank you for the
experience of the psalmist, David, that such depression is
normally only for a short while and that happiness comes in the
morning. In all the business and worry of our daily lives, help
us never to forget to have time for you and with you.   Amen.

224 You have called your people, O Lord, to speak in your name.
We thank you for the wonderful example of men of old like
Abraham and Joseph, like the Lord Jesus himself and his
apostles. We ask now that you will help us to become
ambassadors for Christ, that through our sharing of the good
news, men and women, boys and girls may come to know Jesus

as their Saviour and the forgiveness of their sins, which he brings.
We ask it in his name.   Amen.

Day 16

Jan	Genesis 13:1–9	*May*	Proverbs 10:1–12	*Sep*	Psalm 115:1–13
Feb	Luke 4:38–44	*Jun*	2 Corinthians	*Oct*	Acts 5:33–42
Mar	Luke 22:31–38		6:14–18	*Nov*	1 Peter 1:22–2:3
Apr	Psalm 32	*Jul*	Genesis 41:25–32	*Dec*	Isaiah 40:1–5
		Aug	Luke 11:1–13		

225 Help us to come to you like spiritual babies craving the spiritual
milk of the Bible, just as babies crave for milk to drink. From
its teaching may we learn to uncover our sins to you, that they
may be forgiven. May we be spared the terrible danger of denying
you as Peter once did and may we be always faithful in prayer.
We ask it, heavenly Father, in Jesus' name.   Amen.

226 We thank you, gracious Father, for the wonderful wisdom that
you have given to mankind. We think of men like Abraham,
Joseph and Gamaliel in the Bible. More recently, we remember
men and women of the arts and music who bring joy to our
lives, and of education, medicine and science who help relieve
disease and drudgery for many people. We ask that you will
continue to raise up those who will help to make this world a
happier and safer place to live in; for the glory of your
name.   Amen.

Day 17

Jan	Genesis 13:10–18	*May*	Proverbs 10:13–21	*Sep*	Psalm 119:9–16
Feb	Luke 5:1–11	*Jun*	2 Corinthians	*Oct*	Acts 6:1–7
Mar	Luke 22:39–46		9:6–15	*Nov*	1 Peter 2:13–17
Apr	Psalm 37:1–11	*Jul*	Genesis 41:33–40	*Dec*	Isaiah 40:6–11
		Aug	Luke 11:33–36		

227 Today we ask, heavenly Father, that we may hide your word in
our hearts that we may not sin against you. Particularly we ask

that we may not be jealous of those who live evil lives and yet appear to get away with it. Let us at all times remember that to live in the light of your truth is the only way to being blessed. Amen.

228 We continue to pray for our leaders, Sovereign Lord; for our Queen and her Ministers; for leaders in all walks of life who bear many heavy responsibilities of which we know little. We also pray for those who hold office in the church, for Archbishops and Moderators, and those who serve at our local church/chapel. Help us to make their lives easier in any way we can, by our prayers, our giving and by practical action; in the name of our Servant King, the Lord Jesus Christ. Amen.

Day 18

Jan	Genesis 15:1–6	*May*	Proverbs 10:22–32	*Sep*	Psalm 119:17–24
Feb	Luke 5:17–26	*Jun*	2 Corinthians	*Oct*	Acts 8:26–40
Mar	Luke 22:47–53		12:1–10	*Nov*	1 Peter 3:1–7
Apr	Psalm 40:1–10	*Jul*	Genesis 41:46–57	*Dec*	Isaiah 40:12–17
		Aug	Luke 12:13–21		

229 Open our eyes, gracious Lord, that we may see wonderful things in your law. We thank you that you have saved us from the filth of sin, through Jesus, the Lamb of God, dying in our place on the cross. We thank you that you have reckoned us right with you through faith, set our lives on a rock, assured us that your grace is always enough for us and put a new song in our hearts. In the light of these wonderful truths, may we not fall into selfishness or ever be tempted to betray you. For Jesus' sake. Amen.

230 As a family today we thank you, dear Father, for one another and for your gracious gift of life. We pray that we may always live in harmony with one another, being quick to admit when we are wrong, and ready to say that we are sorry, remembering, as the Family Prayer says, that your forgiveness of us depends

on our forgiving each other. We ask this in your Son's name.   Amen.

Day 19

Jan	Genesis 18:1–10	*May*	Proverbs 11:1–13	*Sep*	Psalm 119:105–112
Feb	Luke 5:27–32	*Jun*	Galatians 5:22–26	*Oct*	Acts 9:1–9
Mar	Luke 22:54–62	*Jul*	Genesis 42:1–17	*Nov*	1 Peter 3:8–12
Apr	Psalm 42	*Aug*	Luke 12:22–34	*Dec*	Isaiah 40:18–24

231 Our great and loving Father, we thank you for your wonderful supply of all the needs of your children: for the gift of a son to Abraham and Sarah, for food for Jacob and his sons in Egypt, for your word as a lamp to our feet and a light for our paths. So deliver us from being downcast and worrying about our feathers, nests and worm supply, remembering that if you care for the birds you will not forget us. In Jesus' name.   Amen.

232 We thank you, gracious Lord, for the amazing way in which you called Levi and Saul of Tarsus to yourself; for the inspired writing they did, as we find it in Matthew's Gospel and the letters of St Paul. We pray that as the lovely fruit of the Spirit grew in those men's lives, so they may grow in ours: the fruit of love, joy, peace, patience, kindness, goodness, faithfulness, gentleness and self-control. For Jesus' sake.   Amen.

Day 20

Jan	Genesis 21:1–8	*May*	Proverbs 12:1–12	*Sep*	Psalm 121
Feb	Luke 5:33–38	*Jun*	Galatians 6:7–10	*Oct*	Acts 9:10–19
Mar	Luke 22:63–71	*Jul*	Genesis 42:18–28	*Nov*	1 John 1:1–4
Apr	Psalm 46	*Aug*	Luke 13:1–9	*Dec*	Isaiah 40:25–31

233 We rejoice, almighty Lord, that you are our refuge; that you give strength to the weary and increase the power of the weak; that you watch over us at all times, never slumbering or sleeping. May we go out from this home into the world today, knowing that you will watch over our coming and going, both now and for ever more.   Amen.

234 Keep us mindful of some of the harder truths of the Bible: that the unrepentant will perish and that we will reap what we sow in our lives. Keep before us, too, the memory of all that Jesus, our Saviour, suffered for us, going through a mockery of a trial before that appalling horror of crucifixion. In his name.   Amen.

Day 21

Jan	Genesis 22:1–8	*May*	Proverbs 12:13–28	*Sep*	Psalm 122
Feb	Luke 6:1–11	*Jun*	Ephesians 5:15–21	*Oct*	Acts 9:20–31
Mar	Luke 23:1–12	*Jul*	Genesis 42:29–38	*Nov*	1 John 1:5–10
Apr	Psalm 47	*Aug*	Luke 13:10–17	*Dec*	Isaiah 53:3–12

235 We clap our hands for joy, O Lord Most High, and thank you that though you restrained Abraham's hand so that he did not sacrifice his only son, Isaac, yet you did not stay your hand when your only Son, Jesus, was to be sacrificed. Instead you allowed the sins and iniquities of us all to be laid upon him.

   In the light of your great mercy, help us to be very careful how we live. Continually fill us with your Spirit, that we may always give thanks to you for everything; in the name of our Lord Jesus Christ.   Amen.

236 We thank you, Lord, that you have ordered your creation to have regular periods of rest each week, not to be a burden, but for worship, leisure and family time together. Help us never to neglect to enjoy this blessed gift of yours that you have intended for our good. And help us to do all we can to ensure that others can enjoy this benefit too. For the honour of your name.   Amen.

Day 22

Jan	Genesis 22:9–18	*May*	Proverbs 13:1–12	*Sep*	Psalm 123
Feb	Luke 6:12–19	*Jun*	Ephesians 5:22–33	*Oct*	Acts 9:32–43
Mar	Luke 23:13–25	*Jul*	Genesis 43:1–10	*Nov*	1 John 2:12–17
Apr	Psalm 48	*Aug*	Luke 14:1–11	*Dec*	Isaiah 60:1–3

237 We pray for the different relationships within our homes, that husbands may sincerely aim to show that same love for wives that Jesus showed for his church when he went to the cross.

May wives submit to husbands, as to the Lord, knowing they have nothing to fear from those who offer them Calvary love in return.

May we all submit our lives to you, heavenly Master, that you may have mercy on us.   Amen.

238 We thank you, heavenly Father, that you have chosen us to be your disciples today. May we not be tempted to follow the ways of a godless world that does not believe in you. Help us to have the reputation of always doing good and having a concern for the poor and oppressed. We ask this in the name of the One who constantly did these things, Jesus Christ our Lord.   Amen.

Day 23

Jan	Genesis 24:1–11	*May*	Proverbs 13:13–25	*Sep*	Psalm 126
Feb	Luke 6:27–36	*Jun*	Ephesians 6:1–4	*Oct*	Acts 10:1–8
Mar	Luke 23:26–34	*Jul*	Genesis 43:11–23	*Nov*	1 John 4:15–21
Apr	Psalm 49	*Aug*	Luke 14:15–24	*Dec*	Micah 5:2–4

239 We were praying yesterday, heavenly Father, about our family relationships. Today we especially think about parents and children. Help us, as parents, to have time for our children, providing time to listen to them and playing our part in training them in the ways of the Lord.

As children, help us to honour our parents, that it may go well with us, and help us to accept that sometimes it may be necessary to receive discipline from their hand. We ask it in the name of Jesus, who knew what it was like to be brought up in a godly home, and was obedient to his heavenly Father even unto death on the cross.   Amen.

240 We know, O God, that your name is Love, and you have shown your love supremely in sending your Son into all the squalor of

the world in the Bethlehem stable, and later to die on the cross
at Calvary, praying that his enemies might be forgiven.

Grant to us grace that we may show this supreme virtue of
love in our lives, by seeking to love our enemies as Jesus taught
us, and recognising that we cannot say we love you without
showing practical love for our fellow creatures.

Guard us from putting the pursuit of earthly riches before
our pursuit of your kingdom and its treasures; for your love's
sake.   Amen.

Day 24

Jan	Genesis 24:12–33	*May*	Proverbs 14:26–34	*Sep*	Psalm 127
Feb	Luke 6:37–42	*Jun*	Ephesians 6:10–20	*Oct*	Acts 10:9–23a
Mar	Luke 23:35–43	*Jul*	Genesis 43:24–34	*Nov*	Revelation 1:4–11
Apr	Psalm 51:1–9	*Aug*	Luke 14:25–35	*Dec*	Isaiah 9:2, 6–7

241 We thank you, gracious Father, for the wonderful way in which
you guide your people. We think especially of how you led
Abraham's servant to find the right bride for Isaac, the penitent
thief to recognise the truth concerning Jesus, Peter to see that
you were opening the kingdom to Gentiles as well as Jews, and
Isaiah and John to foretell the coming of your Son.

Guide us as we go out into the world today, that we may
follow the path of a true disciple; for Jesus' sake.   Amen.

242 We know, heavenly Father, that unless you are the builder of
our house, we work in vain, but if we reverence you our home
will be a secure fortress and a refuge. We pray that we may
never be ashamed to know that you are the unseen Guest at our
table, and the silent Listener to all our conversation.

In our daily walk with you may there be truth in our innermost
parts and may we be clothed with the whole of the Christian
armour that we may not sin against you; for your name's
sake.   Amen.

Day 25

Jan	Genesis 24:50–61	*May*	Proverbs 31:10–23	*Sep*	Psalm 128
Feb	Luke 6:43–49	*Jun*	Philippians 2:5–11	*Oct*	Acts 10:23b–33
Mar	Luke 23:44–49	*Jul*	Genesis 44:1–17	*Nov*	Revelation 2:1–7
Apr	Psalm 51:10–17	*Aug*	Luke 15:1–10	*Dec*	Matthew 1:18–25

243   We thank you, O Lord, that your Son was called Jesus, because he came to save his people from their sins. We thank you for his amazing humility; that he took the nature of a servant and became obedient to death—even death on a cross! We thank you that you have raised him to the place of supreme honour at your right hand on high.

     Grant that we might come humbly before you admitting that, like sheep, we so easily go astray, repenting of our sins and asking that you will create in us new hearts which fear you, and bring further rejoicing in heaven.   Amen.

244   We thank you, Lord, for wives and mothers on whom the main work of the home usually falls. We thank you for their love and considerations, for the hours they spend in providing for our food, clothing, health, and all that goes towards a happy family. Help us to see ways in which we can make their lives easier by our thoughtfulness and prayer. In Jesus' name.   Amen.

Day 26

Jan	Genesis 24:62–67	*May*	Proverbs 31:24–31	*Sep*	Psalm 130
Feb	Luke 7:1–10	*Jun*	Philippians 4:4–13	*Oct*	Acts 10:34–48
Mar	Luke 23:50–56	*Jul*	Genesis 44:18–34	*Nov*	Revelation 3:1–6
Apr	Psalm 53	*Aug*	Luke 15:11–24	*Dec*	Acts 7:54–60

245   As we remember, O Lord, all those who have suffered for their faith in you—those who will have an honoured place in the Book of Life, like Stephen, the first Christian martyr—we pray for all those who suffer for their faith today. Grant them the patience of the psalmist who, out of the depths of his despair, still had hope. Grant, too, that same ability given to your

servant, Paul, who even in prison learned to be content whatever the circumstances. Grant us to be thankful for your many mercies and rejoice in you at all times. For your name's sake.   Amen.

246 We thank you for the wonderful men of faith in the Bible, like the centurion, who so recognised the unique authority of Jesus that he not only had his prayer answered, but received the Master's special commendation. We think too of the courage and faith of Joseph of Arimathea, who never agreed to the death of Jesus, but asked Pilate for the Lord's body. Further, we thank you for the bravery of Peter to bring the gospel to the house of Cornelius, the Gentile. Grant that we may go out into this day with a similar faith and courage to stand up for what we believe. For the honour of Jesus, in whose name we pray.   Amen.

Day 27

Jan	Genesis 25:19–26	*May*	Ecclesiastes 3:1–14	*Sep*	Psalm 139:1–12
Feb	Luke 7:11–17	*Jun*	Colossians 3:1–7	*Oct*	Acts 11:19–24
Mar	Luke 24:1–12	*Jul*	Genesis 45:1–15	*Nov*	Revelation 3:7–13
Apr	Psalm 61	*Aug*	Luke 15:25–31	*Dec*	John 21:20–25

247 As we come to you in prayer today, Lord God, we are aware that you know how we spend our time. Neither darkness nor distance can hide us from your all-searching eyes. You know all about our family life. We pray that it may be marked by the wonderful forgiveness that Joseph showed for his brothers, in spite of the way he was treated by them. We pray that it will not be marred by nasty jealousy such as that between the two brothers in Jesus' story of the lost son who came home. Help us to learn lessons from these stories to apply to our own family; for your name's sake.   Amen.

248 We thank you, living God, that at the very heart of the Bible story is the triumphant resurrection of Jesus from the dead. Therefore we need not fear death, but rejoice that our lives are hidden with Jesus in you. Help us each day neither to think

of, nor do, evil things, but may all our lives be preparing us for our heavenly home, where we will reign with Jesus in glory for ever. We ask it in the glorious name of our Lord and Saviour.   Amen.

Day 28

Jan	Genesis 25:27–34	*May*	Ecclesiastes 11:1–6	*Sep*	Psalm 139:13–24
Feb	Luke 7:36–50	*Jun*	Colossians 3:12–17	*Oct*	Acts 11:25–30
Mar	Luke 24:13–24	*Jul*	Genesis 45:16–28	*Nov*	Revelation 3:14–22
Apr	Psalm 62	*Aug*	Luke 16:10–15	*Dec*	Matthew 2:13–18

249 We confess that we find some things in the Bible story very hard to understand, such as Jacob tricking his brother, Esau, into selling his birthright, the innocent babies having to be killed by King Herod's soldiers, and supremely that Jesus had to die on the cross. Just as Jesus helped those two on the road to Emmaus to understand the Scriptures better, may he, through the Holy Spirit, help us today. We ask it in Jesus' name.   Amen.

250 We thank you, heavenly Father, for the worship and fellowship of the church we attend. We pray that it may always be comparing its life with that of the early church: being ready to repent of and change what is wrong, ready to welcome outsiders, ready to bear with each other and forgive one another, but supremely to be striving to be known for its love. Help us as a family to play our part in this too. For Jesus' sake.   Amen.

Day 29

Jan	Genesis 27:1–10	*May*	Ecclesiastes 11:7–10	*Sep*	Psalm 142
Feb	Luke 7:29–35	*Jun*	1 Thessalonians	*Oct*	Acts 12:1–10
Mar	Luke 24: 25–35		4:13–18	*Nov*	Revelation 21:1–7
Apr	Psalm 65	*Jul*	Genesis 46:1–7	*Dec*	John 1:1–9
		Aug	Luke 16:19–31		

251 Almighty God, we see that the Bible brings us down to earth and shows us that side of life from which we need to be saved.

We think of the blatant favouritism in the home of Isaac and Rebecca, Jacob and Esau; the awful selfishness in the rich man's house; the callous hatred of Christians by Herod, putting some to death to bring him popularity. We thank you, therefore, for the wonderful message of Scripture that true life has come in the Lord Jesus; that at a time known only to you, he will come and gather all believers into one, and that the new heaven and new earth will be revealed. You will wipe away every tear. There will be no more death, mourning, crying or pain, for the old sinful order of things will have passed away. Alleluia!   Amen.

252 We thank you, heavenly Father, for the wonderful love that the Lord Jesus obviously had for everyone, but perhaps especially for young children. How he loved to take them in his arms and bless them. We think of the way he watched children at play and used their games to bring home truths to grown-ups. May we all be humble enough to learn lessons from those younger than we are too. We ask it in Jesus' name.   Amen.

Day 30

Jan	Genesis 27:11–29	*May*	Ecclesiastes 12:1–8	*Sep*	Psalm 150
		Jun	1 Thessalonians	*Oct*	Acts 12:11–17
Mar	Luke 24:36–43		5:1–11	*Nov*	Revelation
Apr	Psalm 67	*Jul*	Genesis 47:1–12		22:12–21
		Aug	Luke 17:1–10	*Dec*	John 1:10–18

253 We bring our praises to you, almighty Lord, for all your mercy and grace towards us, thanking you above all else for revealing yourself to us in the Lord Jesus, who came to our world full of grace and truth. We thank you that he rose physically from the tomb and even ate fish before his astonished disciples. We pray that we may so be living our lives that we may be ready to meet him when he comes again. Come, Lord Jesus.   Amen.

254 When we stop to think, eternal Father, we realise that we are all growing older, and may one day be old, with all the problems that can sometimes bring. Help us to have special respect for

those who are advanced in years, learning from the wisdom their long experience of life can bring, never taking advantage of them because of their infirmities, and doing all we can to make their lives easier. We ask this in Jesus' name.   Amen.

Day 31

Jan	Genesis 27:30–40	*May*	Ecclesiastes 12:9–14		
				Oct	Acts 12:18–25
Mar	Luke 24:44–53	*Jul*	Genesis 50:15–26		
		Aug	Luke 17:11–18	*Dec*	Titus 2:11–14

255 We know, almighty Father, that before you all our lives are open books, and nothing can be hidden from you. Grant us, therefore, to have a healthy fear of your name. Cause us to recognise that although you have a plan for our lives, that does not mean that we may not have to suffer. Help us to follow the example of the leper in the Bible, who returned to give thanks for his healing, by being grateful for your many mercies. May we show forth our thanks by the way we live, both as a family in our home and as witnesses to you in the world outside. For the glory of Jesus Christ.   Amen.

256 We thank you, gracious Father, that after the ascension of your Son the apostles were assured by the angels of his return. Help us to behave in a way that shows we believe the angelic message: by saying 'no' to all that is wrong, and living self-controlled, upright lives as we wait for that blessed hope—that glorious appearing of our great God and Saviour, Jesus Christ. We pray this in his triumphant name.   Amen.

3

Prayers at Festivals

Advent

257 Heavenly Father, as life in our home becomes so busy with all the preparation for Christmas, help us not to become so smothered by the trappings and the tinsel, the cards and presents, the holly and mince pies, that we forget we are celebrating the coming of Jesus, the Son of God, into his world. Make these weeks a time to prepare ourselves for that great day when he will come again in all his glory as Saviour and Judge. We ask it in his name.   Amen.

(Michael Botting)

Christmas

258 Heavenly Father, whose blessed Son shared at Nazareth the life of an earthly home, help us to live as the holy family, united in love and obedience, and bring us at last to our home in heaven; through Jesus Christ our Lord.   Amen.

*(Alternative Service Book 1980
Collect for Christmas 2)*

259 Lord Jesus, we thank you that happiness lies more in giving than in receiving, and that it was for the joy that was before you that you gave yourself upon the cross. Help us to find our

true happiness this Christmas time and always in willing service
for you and those you came to save.   Amen.

(Family Worship, revised)

260   Loving Father, whose Son was born in a stable, and who grew
up to heal the sick and comfort the sad, give us his concern for
the hungry and the homeless, the troubled and the poor. Grant
to all the needy this Christmas, especially those we know and
could help, the knowledge that you sympathise with them in
their distress and the assurance that you hear their prayers;
through Jesus Christ our Saviour.   Amen.

(Adapted from Family Worship)

The turn of the year

261   Heavenly Father, as we enter a new year we look back with
thanksgiving for all your blessings upon our family. We confess
we have not always loved you or one another as we should. We
ask you not only to forgive us, but to give us the will to change
for the better in the year before us. Especially give us grace
within our family to make allowances for our differences in age,
and prepare us for that eternal world where time and age are no
more; for Jesus' sake.   Amen.

(Michael Botting)

Epiphany

262   Lord Jesus Christ, wise men from the East worshipped and
adored you; they brought you gifts of gold, incense, and myrrh.
    We too have seen your glory, but we have often turned
away.
    We too have gifts, but we have not fully used them or offered
them to you.
    We too have acclaimed you as King, but we have not served
you with all our strength.
    We too have acknowledged you as God, but we have not
desired holiness.

We too have welcomed you as Saviour, but we have failed to tell others of your grace.

Lord, in your mercy, forgive us and help us. Make our trust more certain, our love more real and our worship more acceptable; for your glory's sake. Amen.

(Adapted from Church Family Worship, 94)

Palm Sunday

263 Lord Jesus, we remember how fickle the crowds were that first Holy Week: welcoming you on Palm Sunday, crying for your blood on Good Friday. Help us not to condemn them, but acknowledge how prone we are to the same infidelity. Grant us grace to make our praises genuine, our hearts loving and our lives your eternal home; for your name's sake. Amen.

(Michael Botting)

Good Friday

(Prayers based on the seven words of Jesus from the cross.)

(1) 'FATHER, FORGIVE THEM'

264 Sinless Lord, you prayed for the forgiveness of those who drove nails into your hands and feet.

Help us sinners to grasp the immensity of your love and the triviality of the wrongs inflicted on us, and to forgive as you did. For your sake. Amen.

(Michael Botting)

(2) 'WITH ME IN PARADISE'

265 Merciful Lord, you promised paradise to a penitent thief.

Help us sinners to grasp the reality of your love and forgiveness to those who repent, and share the message of your mercy with those who think life is hopeless. For your sake. Amen.

(Michael Botting)

(3) 'BEHOLD YOUR SON! BEHOLD YOUR MOTHER!'

266 Compassionate Lord, you made provision for your mother when
     others provided nothing but pain and suffering for you.

     Help us sinners to forget our own troubles and dedicate
     ourselves to the relief of others. For your sake. Amen.

                                                      (*Michael Botting*)

(4) 'FORSAKEN ME?'

267 Long-suffering Lord, you bore the dereliction of hell that we
     might know the rapture of heaven.

     Help us sinners to spare no effort to bring the good news of
     your sacrifice to a world otherwise without hope. For your
     sake. Amen.

                                                      (*Michael Botting*)

(5) 'I AM THIRSTY'

268 Suffering Lord, you thirsted for us on the cross that the longings
     of our souls might be satisfied.

     Help us sinners to thirst after you and your righteousness, that
     your passion may not have been in vain. For your sake. Amen.

                                                      (*Michael Botting*)

(6) 'FINISHED!'

269 Victorious Lord, you accomplished on the cross our complete
     redemption.

     Help us sinners not only to receive your salvation, but to
     work out its consequences in our daily lives with awe and
     reverence, knowing that it will be completed when you return
     in triumph on the last day. For your sake. Amen.

                                                      (*Michael Botting*)

(7) 'INTO YOUR HANDS . . .'

270 Eternal Lord, your death on the cross has opened up for us a
     new and living way into the heavenly sanctuary.

     Help us sinners to commit our lives into your hands and face
     death with your confidence. For your sake. Amen.

                                                      (*Michael Botting*)

Easter Day

271 Lord Jesus, our risen Saviour, we rejoice in your mighty victory
over sin and death: you are the Prince of Life; you are alive for
evermore. Help us to know your presence in our worship together
as a family and in our life together at home. Grant that the
power of your risen life may be seen when we go out into the
world, and others may want to discover it for themselves. For
your name's sake.   Amen.

(Adapted from Family Worship)

Ascension Day

272 Jesus, King of the universe, as we remember your ascending to
the Father's throne on high to take control of all things, help
us to trust you in all the affairs of our family life, especially
when things seem difficult and the way ahead unclear. Grant
that we may know your will and obey it at all times. We ask
this for the honour of your name.   Amen.

(Michael Botting)

Pentecost

273 We praise you, O God, because you gave the Holy Spirit to
the first Christians, making Jesus real to them, teaching them
the truth, giving them power to witness boldly and filling them
with his fruit. Grant that in our family love, joy, peace, patience,
kindness, goodness, faithfulness, gentleness and self-control may
prevail and those around us may take note that we have been
with Jesus, your Son. For his sake.   Amen.

(Michael Botting)

Harvest

274 Dear Father, at this harvest time we especially thank you for
all the food you give us, both from the land and from the sea.
We thank you too for things that we so easily take for granted,

like fresh water to drink and wash in. We especially pray for those parts of the world where people are hungry and do not have enough food; thirsty and without clean water; sick and do not have doctors, nurses or medicine. Help us who have so much to give them what they need. We pray that you will do what we have asked. Thank you, God.   Amen.

(This prayer is based on themes from prayers sent in by children from Richard Hill Church of England [Aided] Primary School, Thurcaston, Leicester.)

Spring

275 Lord, thank you for all the new life we see in springtime: the blossom on the trees, the bulbs shooting up crocuses and daffodils, the young lambs skipping over the hillsides. Thank you that these signs of life remind us of the new life that Jesus made possible when he was raised to newness of life on Easter Day.

    Grant that we might know that springtime in our lives; for Jesus' sake.   Amen.

(Michael Botting)

Summer

276 Lord, thank you for the summertime when we can enjoy the beauty of the world, especially on country walks, or spending holidays by the seaside or travelling to faraway places. Help us to remember that it was because of your love for us that you made the world. May we respond by helping others to enjoy it and not spoiling it for future generations. For your sake.   Amen.

(Michael Botting)

Autumn

277 Lord, thank you for the wind that blows my cheeks. Thank you for the cold nights with bonfires to keep us warm. Thank you for the grass with dew on it in the morning, when I wake up.

Thank you for the autumn, when the leaves fall off the trees. Thank you for the fruit we pick to eat and make jam with.   Amen.

(Amelia Stockdale, Chester, aged 7)

Winter

278 Lord, thank you for the special treats of wintertime: for the excitement of Christmas and the beauty of frost and snow in the countryside. Help us to remember that winter is also a time when there is more illness around and that bad weather can bring difficulties for the old and those who live in remote places. Enable us to show our love for you by doing all we can to help those in need; for Jesus' sake.   Amen.

(Michael Botting)

A marriage in the family

279 God of love, from whom comes every good and perfect gift, bless M and N whom you join together in marriage today.

May their home be radiant with joy and peace, and may all that is good and pure grow within its walls.

Give them wisdom for the daily affairs of life; bless them in time to come in the ordering of their family; and keep them in their going out and in their coming in; through Jesus Christ our Lord, who with his presence blessed the marriage at Cana.   Amen.

(Adapted from an anonymous prayer in New Parish Prayers, 329)

A birth in the family

280 Heavenly Father, we acknowledge you as the very Creator of life itself, the One who brought joy to the world, through the birth of your only Son to Mary in the little town of Bethlehem. Today we bless you for the joy you have brought to our family through the birth of N. Grant special wisdom to all those who have the responsibility of bringing him/her up. May he/she come to know Jesus as Lord and Saviour and serve him all his/her days; to the glory of your name.   Amen.

(Michael Botting)

Birthday

281   Almighty Creator and heavenly Father, on this our birthday we praise you for creating us and caring for us until now. Help us always to be thankful for the gift of life, and use us every day in your happy service; through Jesus Christ our Saviour.   Amen.

(Family Worship, revised)

4

Miscellaneous Family Prayers and Thanksgivings

Christian marriage

282 We thank you, God our Father,
for the joys of Christian marriage:
for the physical pleasure of bodily union,
for the rich experience of mutual companionship and family life,
and the spiritual ecstasy of knowing and serving Christ together.
Help us to respond to your goodness
by recognising you as Head of our home,
submitting to one another out of reverence for Christ,
bringing up our children in faith and godly fear,
and offering hospitality to the homeless.
We ask this in the name of Jesus our Lord.   Amen.

(Michael Botting)

Family life

283 Father of all, accept our thanks for the joys of family life.

Help us to live so that we may strengthen and enrich the life
of the family.

Help us to build with you the kind of family which welcomes
the stranger, the lonely and the needy.

Teach us through this small family to love the family of all mankind and to realise our part in it.

In the name of Christ we ask this.   Amen.

(Brother John Charles, SSF, Contemporary Parish Prayers, 374)

284 Heavenly Father, we bring to you in our prayers
all whom we love in our family circle,
knowing that your love for them
is so much greater than ours,
and that your will for them
is all that is for their good.
So have them in your keeping, O Lord,
and give them now and always
the fullness of your blessing;
for Jesus Christ's sake.   Amen.

(Frank Colquhoun, Contemporary Parish Prayers, 375)

285 God our Father, be with us in our homes through this and every day.

Help us, when we are tired, to control our wills and tempers and to take thought for others.

Make us loving and patient, forgiving others as we hope to be forgiven; that in our homes your royal law of love may reign; through Jesus Christ our Lord.   Amen.

(James M. Todd, Contemporary Parish Prayers, 376)

Blessing of a home

286 Heavenly Father, whose Son made his home among us here on earth, help us to recognise his presence in this home of ours which we now dedicate to your service.

Let love abound within its walls.

Grant that in every activity we may have the seal of your approval.

May all who visit us here find a haven of joy and peace; and may this home be a foretaste of the eternal home which our Lord Jesus has gone to prepare for us, where we shall be with him for evermore.   Amen.

(Martin Parsons, New Parish Prayers, 336)

287 Most gracious Father,
this is our home;
let your peace rest upon it.
Let love abide here,
   love of one another,
   love of mankind,
   love of life itself,
   and love of God.
Let us remember
that as many hands build a house
so many hearts make a home.   Amen.

(Hugh Blackburne, New Parish Prayers, 337)

Absent members of the family

288 Heavenly Father, you are present everywhere
and care for all your children.
We commend to you the members of our families
who are now parted from us.
Watch over them and protect them from all harm;
surround them and us with your love;
and bring us all at last to that home
where partings are no more;
through Jesus Christ our Lord.   Amen.

(F.W. Street, New Parish Prayers, 345)

One-parent families

289 Loving Father, we ask you to bless fathers and mothers who are
alone in bringing up their families.

Guide and strengthen them when they are beset by doubts
and difficulties; help them to lead their children to know and
love you; and assure them of your presence at all times; for Jesus
Christ's sake.   Amen.

(Mothers' Union Prayer Book)

Our children

290   God our Father, be near to our children growing up in the peril and confusion of these times.

Guard them from the forces of evil at work in our society, and lead them in the paths of goodness and truth; and enable us as parents to give them at all times the security of our love, and the help of our example and our prayers; through Jesus Christ our Lord.   Amen.

(New Parish Prayers, 350)

291   Our heavenly Father,
your Son delighted in the happiness of children.
Bless our children and the children of our affection.
In all things protect and guide their lives;
and as they enjoy the world of your gifts,
grant them the grace of gratitude to you, the Giver;
through Jesus Christ our Lord.   Amen.

(Michael Perry, New Parish Prayers, 353)

(For a marriage in the family and the birth of a baby see previous chapter.)

God's will concerning marriage

292   Heavenly Father, we know that marriage is of your ordaining, and that your Son blessed by his presence the wedding at Cana in Galilee.

But we also learn from his example and teaching that marriage is not your will for everyone.

Grant to each of us personally the knowledge of your will, the grace to accept it, and the power of your Spirit to obey it; for in your will alone we find true peace and fulfilment, and your ultimate glory.   Amen.

(Michael Botting)

Facing retirement

293 Heavenly Father, you have ordained that mankind should both work and rest. We pray for those whose working life is drawing to a close and who are now facing retirement.

Prepare them in mind and spirit for this change in their life's pattern, that their future days and years may be positive and creative, beneficial to the work of the church, and rewarding to all who know them; for Jesus Christ's sake.   Amen.

(Michael Botting)

Sickness in the family

294 Loving and heavenly Father, be especially close to us as a family during this time of illness. We lovingly bring N to you now, that you will grant him/her your peace and bring restoration to full health of body, mind and spirit in your time.

Give to us the faith to believe that whatever may lie ahead you will be with us to strengthen and uphold us, forgiving us our natural anxiety. We ask it in the name of our Saviour and mighty Healer, Jesus Christ our Lord.   Amen.

(Michael Botting)

The loss of a baby

295 Father of all mercies and God of all comfort, whose ways are beyond our present understanding, we lay before you the grievous loss of our baby N.

Be close to us in our grief, and help us to resist the temptation to lose faith.

Make the cloud to lift and the darkness to clear; and through this mysterious tragedy fulfil your loving purpose of us and our family.

We ask it in the name of Jesus, who bowed to your will and trod the way of the cross.   Amen.

(Michael Botting)

Bereavement in the family

296 Loving Father, we know that life's journey sometimes leads through dark valleys, like bereavement, and that many are travelling that path just now, even as we are.

    Help us to remember that however dark the valley, the darkness does not hide us from you. May it not hide you from us, but may we know that you are always near us, sharing our burden and entering into our grief.

    Help us also to remember that the valley will not go on for ever; that with you by our side we shall at length emerge from it, and the darkness will lift, and we shall yet praise you, our Saviour and our God.   Amen.

(Frank Colquhoun, adapted from New Parish Prayers, 521)

Death of a pet

297 Loving heavenly Father, we are all so sad because our pet. . . . (name) has died. We are so pleased that you created him/her for us and gave us so much fun looking after him/her. Thank you for all that he/she meant to us and for all the happy times he/she brought to our home and family. Help us to dry our tears and trust in you when life is sad, as well as when it is happy; for Jesus' sake.   Amen.

(Michael Botting)

Preachers at our church

298 Heavenly Father, thank you for sending Jesus because he taught us a lot through his preaching. I pray for the preachers at my church, for all the effort they put into their work; through Jesus Christ our Lord.   Amen.

(Gemma Waring, Bolton, aged 12)

Thanksgiving for neighbours

299 Thank you, Lord, for the neighbours you have given us,
     as well as the friends we choose.

Thank you, Lord, for people of different ages from us,
as well as those of our own.
Thank you, Lord, for people of different races from us
and of mixed race, as well as our own race.
Help us all to accept each other and serve each other,
recognising that we have all been created in your image,
and offered free salvation through Jesus Christ.   Amen.

(Michael Botting, based on thoughts in a USPG leaflet)

(The following prayers on various themes by children under thirteen were received
by the Editor and have been slightly amended for publication.)

A prayer of commitment

300 Dear Lord, thank you for all the good things you have done for
me. I don't deserve what you gave me at all. I am glad you are
the Lord. I have heard all about you. You should have all the
things you gave me. I don't even deserve to be alive for all the
sins I have done. Will you forgive me for all the sins I have
done? Please come into my life and forgive my sins.   Amen.

(Daniel Gray, Chester, aged 7½)

(This prayer was written during the Billy Graham Livelink Mission in 1989, unknown
at the time by Daniel's parents, without prompting from anyone and completely
unaided.)

The suffering world

301 Dear Lord, we thank you for the beautiful world you have
created. We pray for the people living in the third world. Please
help suffering children to get the love and care they need so
badly. We ask you to help the people suffering from natural
disasters around the world.

Please give us the wisdom we need to look after our precious
planet. We ask this in Jesus' name.   Amen.

(Joel Hockley, Chester, aged 9)

Thanksgiving for creation

302 Thank you for flowers and trees, fish and birds, the planets and
stars. Thank you for mums and dads, brothers, sisters and friends
and, of course, thank you for you and me!
I like leaves and sun and rain and mist and clouds.
I love everything.   Amen.

(Rachel Sarah Cottrell, Marlow, aged 6½)

Holiday thanksgiving

303 Thank you God for tents, for the crabs at the seaside and real
boats. I like the sea and the fish and the sand.
I've been to the seaside. Bye-bye.   Amen.

(Neil James Cottrell, Marlow, aged 3½)

Thanksgiving for school

304 Dear Jesus, thank you for our Sunday school and our church
and our school. Please bless our teachers and the vicar that we
have got at our church. Also bless the helpers and the caretaker
and the dinner ladies. Thank you for the new children who are
coming to our school. Thank you for our writing corner and the
other tables.   Amen.

(Anthony Morgan, Croydon, aged 5)

Miscellaneous children's prayers and thanksgivings

305 Dear God, thank you for families and friends, because life would
be boring without them.
Thank you also for trees and flowers and animals.
Please help the people that are starving and homeless and
those that are dying in hospital.
Please keep us safe, because kidnappers could get us.
Thank you for all the things you give us.   Amen.

(Annemarie Gibson, Northfleet, aged 12)

306 Dear Jesus, sorry for all the bad things that I have done, like being selfish and nasty to my brother and sisters.

Thank you for all the lovely things that you have given us during the summer holidays, especially the sunny weather, visits to the seaside and my birthday party and presents.

Please bless my school and look after all the teachers and children, especially those who are not so lucky as me.   Amen.

(Christine Obee, Gravesend, aged 7)

307 Dear God, thank you for all of the lovely trees and flowers that grow in the garden. Thank you for all of my lovely toys. I have lots of fun playing with them. Thank you for my friends at home and in school. Thank you for my family. Please help me at school.   Amen.

(Claire Cheshire, Gravesend, aged 7)

308 Dear Lord, we thank you for families and friends and things around us. For the trees and the bees. We also thank you for food and drink. And we pray for people that have lost somebody very dear to them and for people that are in hospital.   Amen.

(Sharon Gould, Gravesend, aged 12)

309 Dear Lord Jesus, please take care of all the school children. Help the little ones who have just started school to feel safe and secure as they spend their first days away from their family and homes. Help those who have had to change school to settle in and make new friends, so that they are not lonely. Fill us all with love so that there is no bullying or unkindness.   Amen.

(Hannah Louise Bell, Gravesend, aged 11)

310 Thank you, God, for the lovely world. I like it very much. I think about Jesus being born in his stable; thank you for sending him to us.

I believe in you a lot. Thank you for being with us always.   Amen.

(Lucy Wood, Farnham, aged 6)

311 Thank you, God. Thank you for food and drink.
     Thank you for friends and family.
     Thank you for clothing and warmth.
     Thank you, God, for all the things we have.   Amen.

(Ian Fox-Reynolds, Farnham, aged 10)

312 Dear Lord, we are truly thankful for what we have received from
     you and we are trying to save some of your lovely animals and
     countryside.   Amen.

(Richard Fox-Reynolds, Farnham, aged 8)

313 Dear Father God, thank you for giving us such a beautiful world
     to live in. Thank you we are able to enjoy it.
        Help those people who are so busy fighting over who should
     own different parts of it that they forget how wonderful life is
     in your world, and remind them that they are also taking the
     beauty out of other people's lives.   Amen.

(Elisabeth Cole, Farnham, aged 8)

314 Dear Lord, thank you for all the living creatures you have made,
     like the robins singing outside my window in the morning when
     I lie in bed. And thank you for our new chicken that will soon
     provide eggs for me to have at breakfast time; for horses we can
     ride, and for cows, black and white, that produce milk, cream
     and butter; for puppies that are nice to cuddle and play with,
     and kittens that are warm and furry in my bed at night. Thank
     you, Father, for all these animals that make our lives
     happy.   Amen.

(Anon, Farnham, age under 13)

5

Graces

At a parish lunch

315 Lord Jesus, we remember how you brought blessing to many
meal-times when on earth:
   sharing a wedding feast,
   feeding the five thousand,
   having breakfast by the seaside.
Bless our food and fellowship today.
May this be a time when we experience your risen presence,
and get to know some people better,
and others for the first time;
for your name's sake.   Amen.

(Michael Botting)

At a wedding breakfast

316 For family life, for fellowship and for this food we thank you,
Lord, and ask that we may never be unmindful of the needs of
others. For Christ our Saviour's sake.   Amen.

(Michael Botting)

Graces from former years

317 God bless our meat,
God guide our ways,

God give us grace our Lord to please.
Lord long preserve in peace and health
our gracious Queen Elizabeth.   Amen.

(Anon, 1565)

318 Be present at our table, Lord;
be here and everywhere adored.
Thy creatures bless, and grant that we
may feast in paradise with thee.   Amen.

(John Wesley, 1703–91)

A Scottish grace

319 Some hae meat, and canna eat,
     And some wad eat that want it;
But we hae meat, an' we can eat,
     And sae the Lord be thankit.   Amen.

(Robert Burns, 1759–96)

Breakfast graces

320 For porridge, tea and buttered toast,
Praise Father, Son and Holy Ghost.   Amen.

(Anon—learned at an Anglican Theological College)

321 This is the day the Lord has made,
Thank you for toast and marmalade.   Amen.

(Michael Botting)

322 Praise to God who giveth meat
Convenient unto all who eat:
Praise for tea and buttered toast,
Father, Son and Holy Ghost.   Amen.

(R.L. Gales*)

A grace for ice-cream

323 For water-ices, cheap but good,
  that find us in a thirsty mood;
For ices made of milk or cream
  that slip down smoothly as a dream;
For cornets, sandwiches and pies
  that make the gastric juices rise;
For ices bought in little shops
  or at the kerb from him who stops;
For chanting of the sweet refrain:
  'Vanilla, strawberry or plain?'
We thank thee, Lord, who sendst with heat
  this cool deliciousness to eat. Amen.

(A.M. Laing*)

324 Bless me, O Lord, and let my food
strengthen me to serve you,
for Jesus Christ's sake. Amen.

(The New England Primer, adapted)

325 Come, dear Lord Jesus, be our guest,
and bless what you have given us.
For your name's sake. Amen.

(Adapted from a German grace)

326 You are great and you are good,
And we thank you for this food.
By your hand must all be fed,
And we thank you for this bread. Amen.

(From First Prayers)

327 Bless, dear Lord, my daily food.
Make me strong and make me good. Amen.

(Anon.)

328 We thank you, Father, for your care
        for all your children everywhere.
    As you do feed us all our days
        may all our lives be filled with praise.   Amen.

(Anon.)

329 Thank you for the world so sweet,
    Thank you for the food we eat.
    Thank you for the birds that sing,
    Thank you, God, for everything.   Amen.

(Mrs E. Rutter Leatham)

330 Bless these your gifts, most gracious God
        from whom all goodness springs.
    Make clean our hearts and feed our souls
        with good and joyful things.   Amen.

(Anon.)

331 Lord, bless this food for our use and us in your service, and help
    us to remember the needs of others; for Christ's sake.   Amen.

(Anon.)

Section 3

PRAYERS AT SCHOOL ASSEMBLIES

I

Introduction

When I became Rector of two rural parishes near Chester, it was taken for granted that I would also become Chairman of Governors of the local Church of England Aided Primary School, which was in one of the parishes. I soon discovered that I was also expected to take assembly once a week. This was an opportunity which I came to value, because it gave me the chance to get to know the children—about half of whom lived in the two parishes. However, I am bound to admit that the actual taking of the assemblies I found difficult. To start with, the hymn-book was extremely limited in its range of subjects, and some hymns could have just as easily been sung by children of any faith or none. With the appointment of new staff, this situation changed and we put hymns onto acetates and used an OHP.

However, the major problem was thinking of a new subject every week on which to speak for, at most, five minutes, and to do so in such a way as to retain the children's attention throughout (especially as their ages ranged from about five to thirteen years).

I almost invariably used the question-and-answer method, and found that by very carefully constructing my questions I could sometimes get quite profound answers from even some of the youngest children. I only occasionally used a visual aid, but the overhead projector, latterly used for the hymns, was a useful standby.

The shape of the liturgy was extremely basic: namely a hymn, talk and two or three prayers, followed by a corporate saying of the Lord's Prayer and the Grace.

In producing prayers for school assemblies it seemed appropriate to link them directly to the themes of assembly addresses. As this book is primarily one of prayers, I am not providing full outline talks, but hope that what I have supplied may be sufficient to stimulate ideas, which can be geared either to primary or to secondary school pupils. After each brief outline there follow two prayers on the theme—one designed for the primary assembly and the other for the secondary. Further prayers on more general topics can be found in other parts of the book and an index is provided to help with this.

I have reckoned that there are about forty weeks in the average school year, and I have assumed the academic year begins in September. Themes for the major Christian festivals, therefore, will come roughly in the appropriate places, but with Easter being a moveable feast, I could not be exact.

2

Forty Suggested Themes with Prayers for Primary and Secondary Schools

Theme 1: the new school year

For everyone here something new: school, class-mates and teachers. We would not admit it, but perhaps we are all a little afraid. This term has lots of excitements: harvest, bonfires, Christmas. At the first Christmas the angel of the Lord made four appearances. Can anyone tell me to whom? What were his first words? 'Do not be afraid.' If we trust in God there is no need to fear.

PRIMARY

332 Dear God, for some here they are starting school for the very first time and they feel shy and a little lost and lonely. For all of us some things are going to be new and possibly strange. We all feel a little afraid, but we know we can share our fears with you. Make us all to be friendly and helpful, especially to those who are new, and face the days ahead with courage and excitement; for Jesus' sake.   Amen.

(Michael Botting)

SECONDARY

333 Dear God, entering a new school or new class is another big step in our lives. We know there are going to be many new things to learn and new ways of learning them; there may be much that we shall find difficult. Help us to become neither

discouraged nor self-satisfied, but always to strive to do better and have the courage to take new initiatives. Help us also to stand up for Christian values and not to be ashamed to admit that we follow in the steps of Jesus Christ, in whose name we pray.   Amen.

(Adapted from a prayer by Virginia Salmon)

Theme 2: creation

Refer to our skin: just a piece the size of a normal postage stamp contains four yards of nerves, 100 sweat glands, fifteen oil glands, a yard of blood vessels and three million assorted cells. Quote Psalm 139:14. Light travels at 186,000 miles per second, so to calculate the number of miles in a light year, this has to be multiplied by what? ($60 \times 60 \times 24 \times 365$). The Pole star is 400 light years away, so light we see tonight left it at the time of the Spanish Armada, when Shakespeare was writing plays. Quote Psalm 8:3–4. So size is of no importance to God. He is the God of both infinite detail and infinite power. We are safe in his hands.

PRIMARY

334 Lord of the universe, we praise you for your creation; for the wonder of space, the beauty of the world and the value of earth's resources. Keep us from spoiling these gifts of yours by our selfishness and help us to use them for the good of everyone and the glory of your name.   Amen.

(Family Worship, adapted)

SECONDARY

335 Lord of infinite greatness, you have ordered and adorned in equal perfection all that you have made; you have set in glorious array the eternal heavens, and yet paint the lily that only lasts but a day. Give us courage to attempt great things in your name, and equal faithfulness to do what is small; to your honour and glory alone; through Jesus Christ our Lord.   Amen.

(From Daily Prayer, edited by Eric Milner-White and G.W. Briggs, adapted)

Theme 3: water

Ask questions about something we cannot live without, yet often kills people in some parts of the world. Explain that floods are sometimes the result of mankind's selfishness, cutting down forests, etc. We cannot live only for ourselves, either in school or in the world outside.

End by asking what the especially valuable uses of water are, and be ready to illustrate the answers: cleaning (washing-up bowl), growing (watering can), drinking (tumbler of water). We should never waste it. In some parts of the world people say a prayer of thanksgiving (grace) before drinking it.

PRIMARY

336   Dear Father, we thank you for what we have in this world, like fresh water, fresh food and a good healthy life. We know that in some parts of the world, like Africa, Asia and South America, many people only have very dirty, unhealthy water to drink, in which other people may have had a bath. We pray that we can help these people to have a better life and that you will help us do so.   Amen.

(Based on a prayer by Ruth Lindsey, Cropston, Leicestershire, aged 9)

SECONDARY

337   Jesus Lord and Master, who served your disciples in washing their feet, serve us often, serve us daily, in washing our motives, our ambitions, our actions; that we may share with you in your mission to the world and serve others gladly for your sake; to whom be glory for ever.   Amen.

(Ascribed to Michael Ramsey, Contemporary Parish Prayers, 93)

Theme 4: animals

Who has a pet animal at home? What? Why? How do you think God feels about animals? He made them very good, knows when they die, and does not want oxen muzzled or to go thirsty on the Sabbath. So how should we treat them? Jesus did say, however, that we are far more valuable than sparrows, and he allowed 2,000 pigs to drown so that one man (Legion or Mob) should be delivered. God gave Peter permission to kill and eat animals. So what place should pets have in our lives? Can we learn anything from animals? See Isaiah 1:2–3.

PRIMARY

338 Great Father in heaven, thank you for making animals to be our friends. Give us pity for all sick animals, for hunted and caged animals, for animals that are ill-treated and teased, and for any that are lost and frightened. Make us brave to defend any animal we see being cruelly treated. May we be the friend of all dumb creatures and save us from causing them suffering through our own thoughtlessness.   Amen.

(Brenda Holloway
Prayers for Children and Young People)

SECONDARY

339 Lord, teach us to accept with gratitude and delight the beauty and wonder of the animal creation. You made them, they are yours and you have given them into our hands. Through greed, through selfishness, through curiosity, we woefully misuse them. Change the hearts of everyone, that these things shall not be. Save us from exacting from them too high a price in pain, in order to prolong our lives a little. In laboratory and farm, O Lord, may we be merciful to the helpless; through Jesus Christ our Lord.   Amen.

(Doris Rybot)

Theme 5: harvest—yoke, plough and goad

Ideally have OHP acetate with modern tractor ploughing. Refer back to biblical days when a man drove an ox to plough and have acetate flop-overs that put yoke, plough and goad in place as they are spoken about. Base the talk around the following texts: yoke—Matthew 11:28–30, plough—Luke 9:62 and goad—Acts 26:14. This talk can easily be divided into two, dealing with the goad separately and enlarging on St Paul's conversion.

PRIMARY

340 Creator God, you have provided us with everything we need for life and health. Grant that the resources of the earth may not be hoarded by the selfish or squandered by the foolish, but that all may share your gifts; through our Lord Jesus Christ.   Amen.

(Family Worship, adapted)

SECONDARY

341 In our Christian discipleship, Lord, help us to recognise that none of us can be self-sufficient in this world and none of us needs bear the burdens of life alone. Help us to have the humility to share them with you. Grant us the perseverance to follow you without looking back to the transient pleasures of the world, and respond at once, whenever we are aware of your goading us, to a greater obedience; through Jesus Christ our Lord.   Amen.

(Michael Botting)

Theme 6: loneliness

Ask which torture is thought to be the worst: beating, electric shock, solitary confinement? Explain that loneliness is one of the world's greatest problems. We have many problems and temptations that we feel we cannot share with anyone. Hence explain Hebrews 4:15–16, making reference to Jesus' period in the wilderness when he was also severely tempted. With older pupils, the agony in the Garden of Gethsemane might be used.

PRIMARY

342 Heavenly Father, we know how unhappy we are when we are lonely. Today we especially think of lonely people: those who live alone and find it difficult to get out; those who are ill in hospital and have few visitors; people in prison. May they know that none is beyond your care, and help us to think of lonely people we could help sometimes; for Jesus Christ's sake.   Amen.

(Michael Botting)

SECONDARY

343 O God of love, present in all places and at all times, pour your Spirit of healing and comfort on every lonely heart. Have pity on those bereft of human love, and on those to whom love has never come. Be to them a strong consolation, an ever-present help; and in the end give them fullness of joy, for the sake of Jesus Christ our Lord.   Amen.

(Frank Colquhoun, from Contemporary Parish Prayers, 379)

Theme 7: the tongue

Refer to a fire that might have occurred locally or been seen on TV. How did it start? Possibly just a spark. What would you say was the most powerful part of your body? If not suggested, refer to the tongue and ask why it is so powerful. Mention the spread of gossip, lies about people, etc. Quote James 3:2–10 and possibly Matthew 12:36–37. See also Proverbs 18:8—Good News Bible. Ask in what good ways we can use our tongues, mentioning encouragement, such as the great speeches of Winston Churchill in the Second World War, the praise of God and others. End with using our tongues to pray, which we will do now.

PRIMARY

344 Lord Jesus, we are sorry that we are so quick to answer back, for you kept silence when men made fun of you and told lies about you. You even prayed for those who nailed you to the cross. Help us to learn from you. We ask it in your name.   Amen.

(Zinnia Bryan)

SECONDARY

345 Heavenly Father, who through your Son warned us that by our words we shall be justified or condemned, we pray for writers, journalists and broadcasters whose words so powerfully influence the life of the nation.

    Help them to recognise in the words they write or speak a power for good or for evil, and to use them responsibly as those who must give an account; through Christ our Lord.   Amen.

(Llewellyn Cumings, New Parish Prayers, 239)

Theme 8: St Luke

Who likes riddles? Who would you say is one of the best known writers in the world in all history? If not named give hints: we only know of two books; he did not sign them, though his name appears in the second. Many parts of the world think about the history he wrote three times a year, and sing the three songs he included every day. He wrote more of the New Testament than anyone else and two of its most famous stories, namely the Prodigal Son and the Good Samaritan. He was, of course, St Luke, who was also doctor to the Apostle Paul and wrote both a Gospel and the Acts of the Apostles. What can we learn from his example? Painstaking excellence in all his work. Perhaps end with:

We are writing a Gospel, and chapter each day,
   in all that we do and all that we say.
People read what we write, whether faithless or true.
Pray what is the Gospel according to you?

PRIMARY

346 O God, the source of life and health, we pray for those who are ill. Give doctors and nurses skill to make them well again, and grant that during their illness they may learn more of your love and care; through Jesus Christ our Lord.   Amen.

(Family Worship)

SECONDARY

347 Almighty God,
      who inspired Luke the Physician
      to proclaim the love and healing power of your Son:
      give your church, by the grace of the Spirit
         and through the medicine of the gospel,
      the same love and power to heal;
      through Jesus Christ our Lord.   Amen.

*(The Alternative Service Book 1980
Collect appointed for St Luke's Day, 18th October)*

Theme 9: All Hallows, Jesus the Light

Explain that Hallowe'en is often associated with the devil, evil and darkness, so as Christians we should not be involved. We follow Jesus, the Light of the World. Hallowe'en is the evening before All Hallow's Day or, as we call it nowadays, All Saints' Day. Ask what a saint is. Explain that everyone whose life has been set apart for Jesus is a saint. As saints we should shine for Jesus.

Produce a table lamp with a 200W (or 150W) bulb in it, but with a small circle of black card between the electric terminals and the bulb. Have the lamp plug obviously not plugged to the power supply. Concealed in a box have a 100W bulb connected in series, with the means to cut the 100W bulb out. Ask what the purpose of a bulb is. If it does not shine it is useless and should be discarded. Christians are made to shine (see Matthew 5:16). Ask if the bulb can shine on its own. Explain that we get our light from Jesus the Light. Refer to sun and moon. Why don't we shine?

Switch on lamp. No light. Why? Not plugged in. Christians must be in touch with Jesus. Plug in. Switch on again. No light. Reveal black disc. Christians cannot shine if there is unconfessed sin. Replace bulb and switch on yet again. A very dim light appears. Explain that the bulb has a secret life where most of the power goes. Christians cannot shine for Jesus if there are other things that take first place. Cut out 100W bulb and switch on once more. The light from the bulb will startle everyone. So should Christians. (Based on Talk 41 in my book *Teaching the Families* [Falcon 1973] by Stephen Trapnell.)

PRIMARY

348 O Lord God, we are all called to be your witnesses and shine for you in the world. Help us to make Jesus our Saviour known to others through our words and our lives, our prayer and our gifts; for his sake. Amen.

(Family Worship, adapted)

SECONDARY

349 Almighty God, we praise your holy name for all the saints throughout the ages who have kept the lamp of faith burning brightly. Grant that we who are following in their steps may

be lit by him who is the light of the world, even your Son our Saviour, Jesus Christ.   Amen.

(William Hampson, More Prayers for Today's Church, 296)

Theme 10: bonfires

Ask who expects to have a bonfire with fireworks on 5th November. Ask the origin of the word 'bonfire'. No one is likely to know. Explain that in Europe, animals were slaughtered before winter if they were not to be kept, sheltered and fed over winter. The meat of the animals was kept and the bones and carcasses burned—hence 'bone fires', which contracted to 'bonfires'.

From that introduction talk briefly about one of the various fires in the Bible, for example, Genesis 22, Exodus 3, 1 Kings 18 and Daniel 3. For an expansion of this theme, see my book *More For All the Family* (Kingsway), Talk 34 by Ray Adams.

PRIMARY

350 Thank you, God, for all the fun of bonfires and the dazzling and coloured lights of fireworks. We know, however, that bonfires and fireworks can be very dangerous. Please keep us safe. Stop us from becoming so excited that we do something foolish, and make us obedient to those in charge. For Jesus' sake.   Amen.

(Michael Botting, adapted from prayers by Zinnia Bryan)

SECONDARY

Guy Fawkes attempted to blow up the English Parliament. Let us pray for our Parliament today.

351 Almighty God, we pray for those engaged in the political life of our nation as Members of Parliament.

Help them to put loyalty to what is right above loyalty to party or class, above popularity or the praise of men and women; and may their only motive be to serve their country and promote the welfare of their fellow citizens.

We ask this for the honour of your holy name.   Amen.

(Frank Colquhoun, adapted from New Parish Prayers, 218)

Theme 11: Remembrance

Refer to November being the month to remember. What? Guy Fawkes and world wars. Ask why people are wearing poppies. Explain that in the First World War men who tried to run to enemy trenches often got mowed down by machine-gun fire and lay dead in fields of Flanders poppies. To help us remember, poppies have been sold since 1921 to raise funds for those still suffering as a result of war. Ask if anyone can think of another important event involving death that we remember by means of a special visual aid. Produce bread and wine, and lead into a brief talk about the death of Jesus and why we should remember it.

PRIMARY

352 Loving Father, we thank you for all those who suffered and died in the world wars to help bring peace on earth. But even more we thank you for the death of the Lord Jesus to save us from our sins and bring us peace with you. In your name.   Amen.

(Michael Botting)

SECONDARY

353 Almighty Father, we remember before you those who sacrificed their lives in the struggle for freedom, and we pray that the justice and peace for which they fought may become established today among the families of the nations. We ask this in him who taught us to pray for the coming of your kingdom on earth as it is in heaven, through Jesus Christ our Lord.   Amen.

(Church Family Worship, 706)

Theme 12: St Andrew the Witness

Ask if anyone likes fishing—or if anyone's dad does. Ask what fishermen do when they have a big catch. Must tell everyone. Any fishermen in the Bible? Single out Andrew and tell how he found Jesus and had to tell his brother Peter (see John 1:35–42). Later Jesus told his disciples they should become 'fishers of men'. Ask what he meant.

History records that Andrew was crucified in Achaia (Greece), but on a diagonal cross. Centuries later, when tales of the fearless fisherman reached Scotland, the warriors proclaimed him as their special saint, and made a flag with a white diagonal cross for the purity of his life, on a background as blue as the seas he had sailed to do his Master's work.

PRIMARY

354 Heavenly Father, we pray for those who have gone to other countries with the good news of Jesus. When their work is difficult and tiring make them strong; when they are lonely and homesick remind them that you are with them; when they are uncertain what to do, guide them, and keep them at all times loving you; for Jesus' sake.   Amen.

(Family Worship)

SECONDARY

355 Almighty God,
     who gave such grace to your apostle Saint Andrew
     that he readily obeyed the call of your Son
         and brought his brother with him:
     give us, who are called by your holy word,
     grace to follow without delay
     and to tell the good news of your kingdom;
     through Jesus Christ our Lord.   Amen.

(The Alternative Service Book 1980
Collect appointed for St Andrew's Day, 30th November)

Theme 13: Advent

Who are we afraid might visit our home when we are all out, or possibly at night when we are all in bed? Do burglars warn us when they are coming? Refer to the season of Advent. What does it mean? Whose coming are we thinking about? Refer to Jesus' first coming and his promise to come again, as the Creeds remind us. The Bible says that he will come like a thief in the night (e.g. 1 Thessalonians 5:2). What does it mean? Explain that obviously he comes as a friend, not as a thief, but how would we want him to find us behaving? Possibly refer briefly to one of the parables in Matthew 25. End with the fact that gunners, who help fire big guns, know that the guns are going off, but they still 'jump'. When Jesus returns we should not be surprised, but we shall all no doubt 'jump'!

PRIMARY

356 Lord Jesus, we thank you for your promise to return to this world, not as a tiny baby but as a triumphant King. Keep us watchful against temptation and joyous in your service; for your name's sake. Amen.

(Family Worship)

SECONDARY

357 Almighty God,
  give us grace to cast away the works of darkness
  and to put on the armour of light,
  now in the time of this mortal life,
  in which your Son Jesus Christ
    came to us in great humility:
  so that on the last day,
  when he shall come again in his glorious majesty
    to judge the living and the dead,
  we may rise to the life immortal;
  through him who is alive and reigns
    with you and the Holy Spirit,
  one God, now and for ever. Amen.

(The Alternative Service Book 1980
Collect appointed for Advent Sunday)

Theme 14: the Bible

Ask what has been described as 'the most valuable thing this world affords', and has been compared to milk (1 Peter 2:2), honey (Psalm 119:103), a mirror (James 1:23–25) and a light (Psalm 119:105). Enlarge briefly on one or all of these, using simple visuals of a bottle of milk, jar of honey, hand mirror and a torch.

Explain to older pupils that in the Church of England the second Sunday in Advent is always known as Bible Sunday, and you will be using the Collect appointed for that day in the prayers.

PRIMARY

358 Heavenly Father, through the Bible you have shown the wonder
of your love for us in Jesus Christ. Help us to understand it
with our minds and apply it in our lives; for his sake.   Amen.

(Family Worship)

SECONDARY

359 Blessed Lord,

who caused all holy Scriptures

to be written for our learning;

help us so to hear them,

to read, mark, learn, and inwardly digest them

that, through patience, and the comfort

of your holy word,

we may embrace and for ever hold fast

the hope of everlasting life,

which you have given us in our Saviour Jesus Christ.   Amen.

(The Alternative Service Book 1980
Collect appointed for the second Sunday in Advent)

(*Note:* No theme is provided for Christmas as the festival is celebrated
out of school term. However, if schools are holding Christingle or
Carol Services, ideas for the former can be obtained from the Children's
Society, Edward Rudolf House, Margery Street, London WC1X 0JL.
Outline talks for either can be found in my books mentioned in the
Bibliography. Prayers can be found in Section 2, Chapter 3 of this
book.)

Theme 15: Epiphany

What two particular events happened to the holy family after Jesus
was born? Ask about the gifts the wise men brought. Explain that
they were both meaningful and useful. Gold spoke of majesty, but
would have been very useful in the long journey and stay in Egypt.
Frankincense (or simply incense) spoke of divinity, because it is used
in worship, but would have been good to burn and keep off the flies.
Myrrh spoke of death, but would make good baby powder. What is

the most useful gift we have that we can give to God? Have we truly
given ourselves?

PRIMARY

360   Lord God, we remember how you led the wise men to Bethlehem
       by the light of a star. Guide us as we travel to the heavenly
       city that we and all people may know Jesus as the true and
       living way; for his name's sake.   Amen.

(Family Worship, slightly adapted)

SECONDARY

361   Lord Jesus, may your light shine upon our way,
       as once it guided the steps of the wise men;
       that we too may be led into your presence
       and worship you,
          the Child of Mary,
          the Word of the Father,
          the King of nations,
          the Saviour of mankind;
       to whom be glory for ever.   Amen.

(Frank Colquhoun, New Parish Prayers, 93, slightly adapted)

Theme 16: questions

What happens in a lot of shops after Christmas? Have any here been
dragged off to the sales? Refer to occasional announcements in the
large stores about lost children. Can anyone think of an occasion when
Jesus was thought to be lost (Luke 2:41–52)? Was he really? What
was he doing in the temple? We all learn by asking questions, at first
of those who know more, but later we may have to search for answers
by our own efforts. Never stop asking questions.

PRIMARY

362   Lord Jesus, I don't know much about you,
       but I am willing to learn;
       and I am ready to give all that I know of myself

to all that I know of you;
and I am willing to go on learning.   Amen.

(Dr Donald Coggan, Prayers for Children and Young People)

SECONDARY

363 O God, we pray that your blessing may rest upon our school and on all who teach and learn here. Help us to do our work with all our might and keep us from slack or lazy ways. May we never stop seeking answers to the important questions about our studies and about life itself.

Make us proud of the school to which we belong and that from it we may go forth to serve you and our fellow human beings; for the sake of Jesus Christ our Lord.   Amen.

(Michael Botting, adapted from an unknown source)

Theme 17: tragedy and disaster

(*Note:* From time to time the world is hit by some terrible tragedy or disaster and people ask why God has allowed it. This question can obviously be in young people's minds too. The following brief outline talk attempts to deal with the problem and, of course, can be used whenever it is particularly relevant. Slightly fuller treatment can be found in my book *More For All the Family* [Kingsway], Talk 20.)

Ask the pupils why they think God allowed (name the recent tragedy or disaster). If possible produce a marionette (i.e. a puppet worked by strings). Show how it works and ask if it can love us. We are not like marionettes or puppets. In the Garden of Eden story our first parents were clearly given free choice, which made them human beings. If God stepped in every time we did something bad or stupid we would become like marionettes, jumping when God pulled the string. Refer to the cross as evidence that God cares. When we do something bad God will forgive; when we are stupid he will help us out of the mess.

PRIMARY

364 Loving Father, we don't fully understand why you allow so many tragedies and disasters to happen in the world. We realise that

often they are caused by men and women's carelessness and selfishness. May such things never let us turn away from you, or stop us believing in your perfect goodness.

Meanwhile, we pray for those who have been hurt by the recent tragedy/disaster, and for those who have lost loved ones. Especially help the doctors, nurses and police whose services are needed now. For Jesus' sake.   Amen.

(Michael Botting)

SECONDARY

365 Most merciful God, in the midst of natural disaster
    we look to you in hope and trust,
    acknowledging that there is much in life
    beyond our present understanding.
    Accept our compassion for the suffering;
    bless those who are working for their relief;
    and show us what we can do to share in their task,
    as servants of Jesus Christ our Lord.   Amen.

(Morning, Noon and Night)

Theme 18: the Apostle Paul

Ask what people think of when they hear 'the Damascus Road' mentioned. An important Jew, Saul of Tarsus, was travelling on this road from Jerusalem to Damascus, a journey of about 150 miles, and taking about six days. Relate the story graphically as found in Acts 9, 22 and 26. Make the points that Saul saw a Vision, heard a Voice and came to a Verdict. He became known as Paul the Apostle, one of the greatest Christians of all time. Ask whether such dramatic changes happen today. Give an example.

PRIMARY

366 Thanks be to you, Lord Jesus Christ, for all the benefits that
    you have given us, for all the pains and insults which you have
    endured for us. Most merciful Saviour, Friend and Brother, may
    we know you more clearly, love you more dearly, and follow

you more nearly, as your servant Paul did, now and ever
more.   Amen.

(St Richard of Chichester, modernised and adapted)

SECONDARY

367   Almighty God,
who caused the light of the gospel
    to shine throughout the world
through the preaching of your servant Saint Paul:
grant that we who celebrate his wonderful conversion
may follow him in bearing witness to your truth;
through Jesus Christ our Lord.   Amen.

*(The Alternative Service Book 1980
Collect appointed for the conversion of St Paul)*

Theme 19: coins

Ask if anyone has a British coin on them. Invite them to look at it.
Refer to the wording: DEI GRATIA REGINA and FID DEF (more
recent coins have D.G.REG F.D.). Younger children will have to be
told the meaning, namely 'By the grace of God, Queen' and 'Defender
of the Faith'. Older pupils might be asked. Mention also the Queen's
head. Read, or have read by a competent reader, Mark 12:13–17.
Ask about whether we should pay taxes when we earn our own living.
Why? Mention that Jesus told us to, and some of the things they
pay for like schools, hospitals and police.

But our coins also speak of God, by the words we have noticed
written on them. The Queen's image is on our coins, but God has
put his image on us. Are we living up to our image?

(Based on an idea by Steven Foster in More For All the Family, Talk 57)

PRIMARY

368   Almighty God, our heavenly Father, we pray for our Queen and
the Royal Family, the members of Parliament and all in
authority; that they may govern our country with wisdom and
understanding and for the good of your church and all people;
through Jesus Christ our Lord.   Amen.

(Family Worship)

SECONDARY

369 O Lord our Governor, bless the leaders of our land, that we
      may be a people at peace among ourselves and a blessing to
      other nations of the earth.

          To our Queen and Government and all in administrative
      authority, grant wisdom and foresight in the exercise of their
      duties, that they may provide for the needs of all our people,
      and fulfil our obligations to the community of nations.

          Teach us all, as citizens of this country, to rely on your
      strength and accept our responsibilities to one another, that we
      may serve you faithfully in our generation and honour your holy
      name; through Jesus Christ our Lord.   Amen.

                              (*Frank Colquhoun, New Parish Prayers, 215*)

Theme 20: temptation 1—introduction

Why have school exams? Why sports competitions? To develop mind
and body. What do we mean by temptation? Where does it come
from? Is it wrong? How do we know it is not? Read Matthew 4:1.
Why was Jesus tempted? Why are we? Possibly tell the story of the
development of the Rolls-Royce engine: other well-known engines
were run and run till they broke down. The R.R. engine was then
especially strengthened so that it did not break down at that point.
When we are tempted and resist, we are that much stronger to resist
next time.

PRIMARY

370 Lord Jesus, we are thinking of you in the desert. We remember
      that for forty days and nights you were tempted there to disobey
      God's will. You know how often we are tempted to do wrong.
      Please show us how to overcome our temptations as you overcame
      your own. Help us to be strong-minded and teach us to banish
      wrong thoughts when they come. Make us true and brave and
      more like you every day.   Amen.

                              (*Brenda Holloway, Prayers for Children and Young People*)

SECONDARY

371 Almighty God,
     whose Son Jesus Christ fasted forty days in the wilderness,
     and was tempted as we are, yet without sin:
     give us grace to discipline ourselves
        in obedience to your Spirit;
     and, as you know our weakness,
     so may we know your power to save;
     through Jesus Christ our Lord.   Amen.

(The Alternative Service Book 1980
Collect appointed for the first Sunday in Lent)

Theme 21: temptation 2—the flesh

Ask how we know about the world around us. What do we call sight,
sound, taste, smell and feelings? Mention that all our senses can be
put to good or bad uses. Ask what senses Jesus was tempted to misuse
when he was being tempted in the wilderness. There is nothing wrong
with eating, but it would have been wrong for Jesus then, because
he was specially preparing for his ministry.

Read Matthew 4:3–4 and ask where the quotation in the passage
came from (i.e. the Bible, though Deuteronomy 8:3 would obviously
be acceptable!). Stress the need to read the Bible regularly so that we
know what God's will is for our lives. Perhaps mention that when
the Queen was crowned she was handed a Bible with the words: 'Here
is wisdom, this is the Royal law, these are the lively oracles of God.'

PRIMARY

372 We thank you, God, for the Bible, which is your message to us.
     We thank you because it is true; because it tells us what Jesus did
     and said; because it explains why he came to die for us; and because
     it shows us how you want us to live. In Jesus' name.   Amen.

(Michael Botting)

SECONDARY

373 Almighty God, whose blessed Son was tempted in every way as
     we are, yet did not sin, grant that by your word and Spirit we

may be enabled to triumph over every evil, and to live no longer for ourselves alone, but for him who died and rose again for us, Jesus Christ our Lord.   Amen.

(Frank Colquhoun, New Parish Prayers, 101)

Theme 22: temptation 3—presumption

What do we mean by law? Is it a good or bad thing? If there is uncertainty in the replies, consider life without a highway code! What do we mean by the laws of nature? Who made these laws? What happens if we ignore them, say by walking off a high cliff? Read Matthew 4:5–7 and explain what Jesus was being tempted to do in order to get a following. But Jesus knew that the children of Israel in the Old Testament were rebuked for asking God to perform signs to prove he was there. Jesus therefore must not do the same. In fact it is very unlikely to have worked, for Jesus did do many miracles, but was crucified. Jesus was always obedient to God's laws and God's will and so must we be too.

PRIMARY

374 Almighty Father, please stop us from taking stupid risks because we think it is funny or clever and will make people take notice of us. Help us take proper care of ourselves, such as when we cross roads. May we at all times try to obey both your natural laws and your commandments. In Jesus' name.   Amen.

(Michael Botting)

SECONDARY

375 Teach us, good Lord, to serve you as you deserve, to give and not to count the cost, to fight and not to heed the wounds, to toil and not to ask for any reward, except that of knowing that we do your will; through Jesus Christ our Lord.   Amen.

(Ignatius Loyola, slightly adapted)

Theme 23: temptation 4—true worship

Who gets pocket-money? What do you spend it on? If you want something very much, what are you prepared to do to get it? Save up? Work? Go without things you normally spend your pocket-money on? Is it worth it? What do we mean by worth? What is worship? Literally, worth-ship. Why should we give God worship? Because he is worth it. Why? Because he made us and sent Jesus to save us from our sins.

Read Matthew 4:8–10. What was the devil asking Jesus to do? Why did Jesus refuse? How should we worship God? When we do wrong, whom are we really worshipping?

PRIMARY

376 Lord Jesus, when you were in the wilderness you disciplined your body; you had the courage to resist temptation and the strength to take the way which led to the cross. Help us, O Lord, to follow your example, that we may be stronger in body and mind, and so be ready and able to take our place in the world.   Amen.

(Nancy Martin, Prayers for Children and Young People)

SECONDARY

377 Almighty God,
    to whom all hearts are open,
    all desires known,
    and from whom no secrets are hidden:
    cleanse the thoughts of our hearts
    by the inspiration of your Holy Spirit,
    that we may perfectly love you,
    and worthily magnify your holy name;
    through Christ our Lord.   Amen.

(Alternative Service Book 1980
Collect for Purity)

Theme 24: April fools

(*Note:* If this talk is not given on 1st April slight adjustment will be necessary.)

Has anyone been made an April fool today/this year? Has anyone made someone else an April fool? Possibly ask how.

There are several references to fools in the Bible. Here's one: read Luke 12:13–21. Why was he a fool? He lived for himself and he seemed to forget that one day he would die. Someone asked how much a millionaire left after he had died. The answer was 'everything'. Shrouds have no pockets! If we only live for ourselves God calls us fools.

PRIMARY

378 Teach us, our Father, to give ourselves to you
      as Jesus did, without being mean or selfish.
Help us to think always of what others need;
help us to share what we have with others.
You have given us so many good things.
We thank you most of all for the love of Jesus,
      the greatest gift of all.   Amen.

(R.S. Macnicol, Prayers for Children and Young People)

SECONDARY

379 Jesus Christ, who taught your disciples to seek first the kingdom of God, help us in our daily lives to remember to put first things first; to think the thoughts that are worth thinking; to do the things that are worth doing, and not to please ourselves. Teach us that in forgetfulness of self, and in ministering to the needs of others, we may be servants for the kingdom of God.   Amen.

(Slightly adapted, Prayers for Children and Young People)

Theme 25: Palm Sunday

(*Note:* Though this day, Easter and Pentecost obviously fall on Sundays when there is no school assembly, there is no reason why these subjects should not be taken, as probably many of the pupils will not be in church on those occasions.)

Who knows what next Sunday is? If you go to church, what might you be given? Read Matthew 21:1–17 getting everyone to take the various parts and you the narrator. Those who cannot take individual parts like Jesus can be part of the crowd (v. 9) or children (v. 15). Ask what the people were trying to make Jesus. Did he want to be their king? What sort of king did he really want to be? How does he want to be our king? He wants to be king over our minds (he taught), king over our worship (God or money).

PRIMARY

380   Lord Jesus, we think of you riding into Jerusalem on a donkey and being given a king's welcome. Yet a few days later the crowd was howling for you to be crucified. Help us to make you the king of our lives and not turn from you if others tease and laugh at us. For your name's sake.   Amen.

(Michael Botting)

SECONDARY

381   Dear Lord and Master,
      you showed the world your princely power
      by riding into Jerusalem on a donkey.
      Grant to us all that even as we rejoice in you as our King,
      we may follow you in your great humility to the cross,
      and so may experience the glory of your victory over sin and
      death.   Amen.

(Alan Warren, New Parish Prayers, 107)

Theme 26: crosses

Ask the pupils for the different ways in which we use a cross sign. Have an OHP with a thin card cross on it that can be moved around according to the replies received, such as addition or multiplication sign, something wrong, red cross, traffic sign, kiss at the end of a letter, etc. Then put on an acetate of the cross of Jesus to the side and have others illustrating something wrong (e.g. an addition sum) and talk about sin; a letter or Valentine card with the words 'I love you' and talk about God's love; a road sign and talk about the need to make a decision about Jesus. (Fuller details can be found in my book *For All the Family* [Kingsway] Talk 22 by John Anscombe.)

PRIMARY

382   Heavenly Father, we thank you for giving your Son to die on the cross that we might be forgiven. Help us to understand the

consequences of our sin and the greatness of his love, so that we may trust him as our Saviour and serve him as our Lord. Amen.

(Family Worship)

SECONDARY

383 Lord Jesus, master carpenter of Nazareth, who on the cross with wood and nail has wrought mankind's full salvation, wield well your tools in this your workshop, that we who come to you rough-hewn, may be fashioned to a fuller beauty by your Holy Spirit; for your name's sake. Amen.

(Anon, adapted)

Theme 27: Easter 1

Do something very extraordinary—something that no one would expect someone leading a school Christian assembly to do, such as shaving. If someone then went outside into the street and told a passing policeman, he would almost certainly dismiss it. But if the entire school then went and said the same, he would be obliged to consider it more seriously. Enlarge on 1 Corinthians 15:6.

PRIMARY

384 Lord Jesus, our risen Saviour, we rejoice in your mighty victory over sin and death. You are the Prince of Life, you are alive for ever more. Help us to know your presence, not only as we worship you here, but at home, and wherever we go; for your great name's sake. Amen.

(Family Worship)

SECONDARY

385 Lord of all life and power,
who through the mighty resurrection of your Son
overcame the old order of sin and death
to make all things new in him:
grant that we, being dead to sin
and alive to you in Jesus Christ,

may reign with him in glory;
to whom with you and the Holy Spirit
be praise and honour, glory and might,
now and in all eternity.   Amen.

*(Alternative Service Book 1980
Collect appointed for Easter Day)*

Theme 28: Easter 2

Why should we believe that Jesus rose from the dead? Mention five reasons very briefly: (1) The Old Testament (Psalm 16:8–11); (2) Jesus said he would (Mark 8:31); (3) His first witness was a woman, Mary Magdalene (John 20:16–18). It is extremely unlikely that this would have been invented, as in those days a woman's testimony would not have been accepted in a law court. (4) The disciples (1 Corinthians 15:5–8). (5) You and me. If we ask the risen Jesus to come into our lives, we come to know that he does.

PRIMARY

386 Jesus, our Lord, we praise you that nothing could keep you
dead in the grave. You are stronger than death and the devil.
Help us to remember that there is nothing to be afraid of,
because you are alive and by our side.   Amen.

(Zinnia Bryan)

SECONDARY

387 O Lord our God, we praise you for bringing the Lord Jesus
Christ back from the dead, and for giving him a place at your
side, far above all kings and rulers. We thank you for making
him our living Saviour, who is always able to keep us from
doing wrong. We thank you that every moment of every day
he lives to pray for us. In his name.   Amen.

(Zinnia Bryan)

Theme 29: St Mark

Ask who likes detective stories. We are going to discover all we can about KOLOBO-DACTYLUS, nickname for John Mark (more later). Hence refer to following texts with brief explanation:

(1) Acts 12:12—most likely the house of the Last Supper, from which the young Mark followed Jesus and the disciples to the Garden of Gethsemane. When Jesus was arrested it is assumed Mark was the young man who fled naked (Mark 14:51), because his is the only Gospel in which it is mentioned, and must have meant something to the author of the Gospel.

(2) Acts 13:13—Mark deserted. There was a law in the Roman Empire that a deserter from the army would have the little finger of his right hand cut off. There is a tradition that Mark cut his own finger off as a constant reminder that he had deserted and so was 'maimed in the finger'—the meaning of the nickname. The Apostle Paul did not trust Mark at first because of his desertion (Acts 15:37–38).

(3) 2 Timothy 4:11—Paul now trusted Mark.

(4) 1 Peter 5:13—it is thought Peter gave Mark a lot of material for his Gospel.

What would be our verdict on KD? Possibly end with the poem concluding Theme 8.

PRIMARY

388 Lord Jesus, we are sorry that we have sometimes done bad things which often hurt other people and especially you. Thank you that you still love us, even though we don't deserve it. Please forgive us and take our sins away. We cannot be good without your help, so please come to our aid when next we are tempted to do wrong. For your name's sake. Amen.

(Michael Botting)

SECONDARY

389 Almighty God,
    you have enlightened your holy church
        through the inspired witness

of your evangelist Saint Mark.
Grant that we, being firmly grounded
in the truth of the gospel,
may be faithful to its teaching
both in word and deed;
through Jesus Christ our Lord.   Amen.

(Alternative Service Book 1980
Collect appointed for St Mark's Day)

Theme 30: Matthew

Ask for names of Jesus' disciples. Who knows any of their jobs? Which one looked after their money? Before following Jesus Matthew was dishonest and unpopular, because he collected taxes for the Romans and took more than he should. Why do you think he followed Jesus when he must have known Jesus stood for goodness, honesty and truth? Do we sometimes feel bad inside—and unpopular? Just as Jesus welcomed Matthew, so he welcomes us to be his followers. When Matthew began following he felt so happy he threw a party for all his friends to meet Jesus, and later wrote a Gospel so that we should meet Jesus too.

(Another talk on Matthew is to be found in my book *More for All the Family* [Kingsway], Talk 75.)

PRIMARY

390 Our Lord God, we thank you for all your blessings, for life and health, for laughter and fun, for all the powers of mind and body, for our homes and the love of dear ones, for everything that is beautiful, good and true; but above all for giving your Son to be our Saviour and Friend. May we always find our true happiness in pleasing you and helping others to know and love you.   Amen.

(Family Worship)

SECONDARY

391 Almighty God,
who through your Son Jesus Christ

called Matthew from selfish pursuit of gain
to become an apostle and evangelist:
free us from all possessiveness and love of riches
that we may follow in the steps of Jesus Christ our Lord;
who is alive and reigns with you and the Holy Spirit,
one God, now and for ever.   Amen.

(Alternative Service Book 1980
Collect appointed for St Matthew's Day)

Theme 31: Ascension

Prepare three large envelopes each addressed to 'A. Pupil' followed
by the address of the school. The first letter is for a birthday and the
envelope contains a large cheque marked: 'The Bank of Heaven:
Anytime. Pay: All Christians. Sum: "You will receive power" (Acts
1:8), Jesus Christ.' The second is a royal letter marked 'OHMS'. The
note inside is the command, 'Be my witnesses' (Acts 1:8). The third
letter is private and the contents a card bearing the words, 'This Jesus
. . . will come' (Acts 1:11). Before the talk, arrange for three children
of varying ages to be ready to bring up their envelopes when you ask
for them. Recount briefly the story of the Ascension and explain that
Jesus' last words and the message of the angels were rather like three
letters. Hence comment on each as it is brought up.

(Based on Talk 22 by Garry Guinness in the book *Teaching the
Families*.)

PRIMARY

392 Jesus, King of the universe, thank you for rising to the Father's
      throne on high to take control of all things. Help us to trust
      you when life is difficult and obey you at all times. We ask this
      for the honour of your name.   Amen.

(Family Worship)

SECONDARY

393 Almighty God,
      as we believe your only-begotten Son our Lord Jesus Christ
      to have ascended into the heavens,

so may we also in heart and mind thither ascend
and with him continually dwell;
who is alive and reigns with you and the Holy Spirit,
one God, now and for ever.   Amen.

(Alternative Service Book 1980
Collect appointed for Ascension Day)

Theme 32: the Holy Spirit/Pentecost

Is fire a good thing? Draw out the different ways in which it is
valuable: cooking our food and keeping us warm, providing power
for industry, etc. Who knows what next Sunday is (Whitsun or
Pentecost)? What very important event happened on that day in the
Bible? Hence draw out the coming of God's Holy Spirit with tongues
of fire. In what ways is God's Spirit like fire? He gives us the power
to do what Jesus told us; he warms our hearts with the truth of the
Scriptures (see Luke 24:32). And just as fire purifies our food to make
it fit to eat, so the Holy Spirit purifies our lives that they are more
like Jesus'. End with the story of the Indian smelting precious metals,
like gold and silver, to burn all the impurities away. Ask him how
he knows when the metal is completely pure, and he will say: 'When
I can see my face perfectly reflected in it.' The Holy Spirit wants to
see the face of Jesus reflected in us. Are we trying to quench the Spirit?

PRIMARY

394 We praise you, O God, because you gave the Holy Spirit
to the first Christians, making Jesus real to them, teaching them
the truth and giving them power to witness boldly. Fill us with
the same Spirit that we may know their experience and follow
their example; for Jesus' sake.   Amen.

(Family Worship)

SECONDARY

395 Lord Jesus, we thank you that you have fulfilled your promise
and given us your Spirit to abide with us for ever. Grant us to
know his presence in all its divine fullness.

May the fruit of the Spirit be growing continually in our

lives; may the gifts of the Spirit be distributed among us as he wills to equip us for your service; and may the power of the Spirit be so working in us that the world around may increasingly come to believe in you. We ask it, Lord, in your victorious name. Amen.

(Michael Botting)

Theme 33: Jesus and fun

(*Note:* This talk could be given on a 'fun' or 'red nose' day.)

Do you think Jesus had fun? Do you think he ever laughed? He told us we could be joyful (John 16:20) and one of his greatest followers, the Apostle Paul, told us we should always rejoice (Philippians 4:4). Do you think we can rejoice without laughing? To laugh is all part of being human, so we can be sure Jesus was frequently laughing. But we can get clues from the Gospels by what he said. For example, by telling us not to judge others and trying to take a speck out of their eyes when we have a plank of wood in ours! The story of the man who demanded bread at midnight in Luke 11 on the theme of prayer was surely told with great humour. We can also get a clue from what he did, attending a wedding and making sure the wine did not run out (John 2). He also enjoyed meals with lots of people. Let's all have a good day! Jesus would and will.

PRIMARY

396 Thank you, Lord Jesus, that you have come to bring us eternal life and joy that no one can take from us. Thank you too for the wonderful gift of laughter and fun. However, help us to make sure that our jokes and our fun are both clean and never hurt other people. We especially pray for those not so fortunate as we are: the hungry and homeless, the sick and the bereaved, that their sorrow may be turned into joy; for your name's sake. Amen.

(Michael Botting)

SECONDARY

397 We rejoice, heavenly Father, in the promise that in your Son
Jesus Christ there is perfect freedom and joy.

   In his name we pray for those who are subject to the slavery
of sin, by gambling and betting, by excessive drinking, by
addiction to drugs, and by the misuse of their sexual instincts.
Enable them by the power of your Spirit to overcome these evil
compulsions, and in your mercy grant them the liberty you offer
them in abundance through Jesus Christ our Lord.   Amen.

(Michael Botting)

Theme 34: Peter

Who's keen on cricket or tennis? Have you been watching it on TV?
Did you think some players could do better? Who do you think really
knows most: the players or the spectators? Who knows most of what
it is like to be a Christian? Sometimes Jesus' followers can let him
down. Ask for suggestions to draw out the name of Peter and ask
what he did. He had, of course, been sleeping instead of praying and
then mixing with bad company, so the temptation to deny Jesus was
very much stronger. But when he saw what he had done he was very
sorry and asked for Jesus' forgiveness. Then he got back into the game
and eventually was crucified for standing up for Jesus—tradition says
upside down. Are we spectators or players in the Christian game?

PRIMARY

398 Lord God Almighty, Shaper and Ruler of all creatures, we pray
you of your mercy to guide us to your will, to make our minds
loyal, to strengthen us against temptation, to put far from us
all sinfulness. Shield us against our foes, seen and unseen; teach
us that we may inwardly love you before all things with a clean
mind and a clean body. For you are our Maker and our Saviour,
our help and comfort, our trust and our hope, now and
ever.   Amen.

(Adapted from a prayer by King Alfred, 849–901)

SECONDARY

399 We praise you, Lord Christ, for your apostle Peter, the man of rock:

> for his bold confession of your name;
>
> for his courageous leadership of the apostolic church;
>
> for his abounding zeal in your service;
>
> for his love and loyalty to you, his Lord.

Give us the same rock-like qualities of faith, courage and devotion in your service, and keep us steadfast to the end; for the honour of your great name.   Amen.

(Frank Colquhoun, Contemporary Parish Prayers, 222)

Theme 35: the Lord's Prayer 1—our Father

(*Note:* Today, and for the next three weeks, we consider the Christian Family Prayer. In a sense, this is not the Lord's prayer, for he would not use it for himself, seeing as he never had sins to confess. He taught it to his disciples as a model for their prayer. It is suggested that the modern version of the prayer, found, for example, in the ASB, might be put on an OHP acetate and used each week to help familiarise the school with it.)

Can anyone name some of the special stories Jesus told, which we sometimes call parables? If the Prodigal Son is not mentioned, encourage it to be. Then attempt to draw out the story. What do you think is the most wonderful thing the story is telling us? Enlarge on the marvellous love of the father for his straying son. Apply it to God and ourselves.

Ask how the Lord's Prayer begins. Explain that however good our human fathers are, and tragically some are not good, no human fathers are perfect, but God our Father is perfect, and there is nothing that we need ever be afraid to tell him or ask him, because he loves us so much. Let's talk to him now.

PRIMARY

400 We love you, Father, because you are patient and gentle with us, understanding that we cannot be good without your help, not getting angry with us when we deserve it, loving us all the time whatever we do, always ready to forgive us when we come to say sorry. We thank you in Jesus' name.   Amen.

(Zinnia Bryan)

SECONDARY

401 Father of all, we give you thanks and praise, that when we were still far off you met us in your Son and brought us home. Dying and living, he declared your love, gave us grace, and opened the gate of glory. [May we who share Christ's body live his risen life; we who drink his cup bring life to others; we whom the Spirit lights give light to the world.] Keep us firm in the hope you have set before us, so we and all your children shall be free, and the whole earth live to praise your name; through Christ our Lord.   Amen.

(Alternative Service Book 1980
Rite A Holy Communion Service)

(The section in brackets should be omitted when the occasion is not a Communion Service.)

Theme 36: the Lord's Prayer 2—give us

Ask how many Bible stories can be remembered that mention bread (e.g. wilderness, feeding of four and five thousand, parable of three loaves, Last Supper). What do you think bread represents? Everything we need for physical life. Tell as vividly as possible the story in Luke 11 of the man who woke his neighbour at midnight for some bread. If the neighbour eventually gave him all he needed, how much more will God, our heavenly Father. Keep that in mind when we pray, 'Give us today our daily bread.' Ask what we should especially pray for, and possibly compose an extempore prayer incorporating the requests.

PRIMARY

402 When I am lonely,
      And need a friend,
      My heart is broken and needs a good mend.

I put my hands together,
And close my eyes,
Pray to my God,
The Lord up high.
Oh, Lord Jesus,
Please come to me.
I need your power
Because I am lonely.
Please be with me now,
And for the rest of my days,
In all my doings and all my ways.
Please be my friend among all men.
Thank you, Lord Jesus, my powerful God.   Amen.

(Benjamin White, South Harrow, aged 8½)

SECONDARY

403 Most merciful God, we commend to your care the men, women and children in our world who are suffering anxiety and distress through lack of food.

    Strengthen and support them in their need; and grant that the nations may grow in their concern for one another and in their readiness to share all your gifts; that all may live together in the fellowship, freedom and joy of your kingdom; through Jesus Christ our Lord.   Amen.

(Morning, Noon and Night)

Theme 37: the Lord's Prayer 3 — forgive us

Whether it has been mentioned before or not, this might be the right time to ask why the Lord could not pray what we call the Lord's Prayer. Hence enlarge briefly on how it was essential that he was sinless, or he could not offer his life as a sacrifice for the sins of the world—which he did when he died on the cross. Perhaps quote from Mrs Alexander's hymn 'There is a green hill far away', which could also have been sung earlier in the assembly:

There was no other good enough
to pay the price of sin;

he, only, could unlock the gate
of heaven—and let us in.

Ask whether, because Jesus has died on the cross, we are all forgiven.
Draw out from the Lord's Prayer (which could be on an OHP acetate)
that we have (1) to ask God's forgiveness i.e. own up, and (2) to
forgive others. The second point could be illustrated with the biblical
story of the king who forgave his servant a great debt (Matthew
18:21–35). This story has been amusingly dramatised by Burbridge
and Watts in *Time to Act* (Hodder & Stoughton), pp. 73–77.

PRIMARY

404 Almighty God, we confess that we have sinned against you in
     thought, word and deed: we have not loved you with all our
     heart; we have not loved our neighbours as ourselves. Have
     mercy upon us, cleanse us from our sins, and help us to overcome
     our faults; through Jesus Christ our Lord.   Amen.

(Family Worship)

SECONDARY

405 Dear God, we find it so hard to forgive those who are unkind
     to us, or who blame us for things which are not our fault. We
     go on bearing a grudge against them and even when they try
     to make it up we feel bitter and hard.
         We know this is wrong. When Peter asked Jesus how many
     times he ought to forgive someone who had wronged him, Jesus
     said he must go on and on forgiving. Jesus even prayed for
     forgiveness for those who crucified him. Please help us to be
     more like him and willing to forgive. For Jesus' sake.   Amen.

(Nancy Martin, slightly adapted)

Theme 38: the Lord's Prayer 4—lead us

Have you ever been asked to do something, say by one of your parents
or a teacher, and wondered whether they have ever had to do it? Is
it fair to be asked to do something they've never done? When God
allows each of us to be tempted, we know that he knows all about

temptation himself, because he allowed Jesus to be tempted. When? Mention that it was the Holy Spirit who led Jesus into the wilderness, where God allowed the devil to tempt him. God never leads us into temptation, but he does allow the devil to tempt us. However, the devil wants us to lose the battle, but God wants us to win. Just as Jesus had the Holy Spirit's help, so have we. However, we can do things to help ourselves. Martin Luther, a great German Christian leader of the sixteenth century said, 'You can't stop birds flying over your head, but you can stop them making nests in your hair!' Tell the story of the boy who had been told on no account to bathe in a particular river, because the reeds made it very dangerous. He was later seen returning from the direction of the river carrying his swimming trunks, and was asked if he had been in the river. He denied that he had. 'Why are you carrying your trunks, then?' he was asked. 'Because I thought I might be tempted!' he replied.

PRIMARY

406 Lord Jesus, please stop us from thinking it's funny or clever to be naughty; that it doesn't really matter if we do little things that are wrong. Keep us from feeling that it's all right to do wrong if others are doing it. Please help us not to pretend that we are good. For your sake.   Amen.

(Zinnia Bryan)

SECONDARY

407 Lord, we confess to you what we are: we like the path of life to be easy; we like every step to be free from fear; we like the world to be at our feet. Lord, by all the grace of those forty desert days, arm us against those temptations, alert us to their corruption, forgive us our sins, and teach us to tread the way that Jesus takes; for his sake.   Amen.

(Church Family Worship, 722, slightly adapted)

Theme 39: the Christian race

Refer to the school sports day if there is one taking place around this time, and then say how in the Bible the Christian life is spoken of as a race in various places, such as 1 Corinthians 9:24–26 and Hebrews 12:1–2. (Read in a modern version like Good News Bible.) Ask what similarities can be seen, drawing out the need for discipline, no cheating (sin), spectators to cheer us on and a prize at the end. Perhaps end with the true story of a man who eventually became a great Christian leader and preacher. While a student, he was having coffee with friends late in the evening, when suddenly the host said, 'Do stay, make some more coffee, but I have to go to bed, because I am in training for the race.' The Christian visitor was challenged to realise that his fellow student was doing this for a worldly crown. What was he doing for a heavenly one?

PRIMARY

408 God, give me strength to run this race,
    God, give me power to do the right,
    And courage lasting through the fight.
    God, give strength to see your face,
    And heart to stand till evil cease,
    And at the last, O God, your peace.   Amen.

(Jane Vansittart, slightly adapted, from Prayers for Children and Young People)

SECONDARY

409 We pray, O God, for those who engage in sports and contests, for their own pleasure and the entertainment of others.

    We ask that through their knowledge of the rules of the game they may see that there are greater laws;

    that through their experience of training they may see that there is a greater discipline;

    and that through their desire for victory they may be directed to the greatest triumph of all, and the goal which is Christ, the Saviour of the world. For his name's sake.   Amen.

(Christopher Idle, Contemporary Parish Prayers, 358)

Theme 40: holidays

(*Note:* It is assumed that this talk will be given very close to the end of term.)

What do you especially like doing during the holidays? Hopefully, perhaps encouraged by you, someone will suggest picnics. Ask if anyone can think of a picnic in the Bible and encourage the answer of the feeding of the five thousand. Make reference to: (1) the size of the crowd, which was probably much larger than 5,000, as that may only have referred to the men. Give some idea of a place or ground that would take that number. (2) The smallness of the contribution, which only a small child could carry, of five cheap bread rolls and small fish to flavour them. Even after all had eaten there were twelve baskets of scraps! (3) The secret of the child was that he gave all his picnic to Jesus—something which may have been quite a struggle for a hungry lad to do. Jesus did the rest, and the boy did not go without.

Perhaps end with a story of the cricketer, Victor Trumper, who on going out to bat accepted the invitation to use a small boy's bat, yet still made a great score. The reason? The little bat was in the hands of the master. Are our lives in the hands of the Master?

PRIMARY

410 Heavenly Father, because you rested from your work of creation,
       we thank you for the opportunities we have of holidays and
       leisure. Refresh our bodies, minds and souls so that we may
       return to our daily work better able to serve you; for Jesus'
       sake.   Amen.

(Family Worship)

SECONDARY

411 Heavenly Father, we thank you for all your goodness to us:
             for the wonder of your creation,
             for the happiness of holidays,
             for human love and friendship.
       May we know you better through your Son Jesus,
             and live our lives to your glory
             and in the service of others,
       through the power of your Holy Spirit in us,
             now and always.   Amen.

(Hugh Blackburne, Contemporary Parish Prayers, 679)

Bibliography

(* the book may be out of print)

General

Patterns for Worship, a Report by the Liturgical Commission of the General Synod of the Church of England (CHP).

Frank Colquhoun (ed.), *Contemporary Parish Prayers* (Hodder & Stoughton).

Frank Colquhoun (ed.), *New Parish Prayers* (Hodder & Stoughton).

* Mervyn Peake, *Prayers and Graces* (Pan).

Dick Williams (ed.), *More Prayers for Today's Church* (Kingsway).

Prayers for Uniformed Youth (The Anglican Fellowship), obtainable from the Secretary, Anglican Fellowship, 31 Losely Road, Farncombe, Godalming, Surrey GU7 3RE.

Family Prayers

* Zinnia Bryan, *Let's Talk to God* (Scripture Union).

* Beryl Bye, *Prayers at Breakfast* (Lutterworth).

Frank Colquhoun, *Family Prayers* (Triangle SPCK).

Benjamin Jenks (Peter Toon, ed.), *Prayers for Families* (Hodder & Stoughton).

Michael Perry (ed.), *Church Family Worship* (Hodder & Stoughton).

Paul Simmonds (ed.), *Church Family Worship Resource Book* (CPAS).

Prayers for Younger Children

Helen Gompertz, with illustrations by Vic Mitchell, *First Prayers* (Scripture Union).

The Lion Book of Children's Prayers (Lion).

The Lion Prayer Collection (Lion), edited by Mary Batchelor, over 1000 prayers for all occasions.

David Palmer, *Book of Prayers* (Ladybird).

Tasha Tudor (illustrator), *First Prayers* (Lutterworth). Also, *More Prayers* and *First Graces*.

Prayers for Schools

R.H. Lloyd, *Acts of Worship for Assemblies*, Vols 1–3 (Mowbray).

R.H. Lloyd, *Assemblies for School and Children's Church* (Mowbray).

R.H. Lloyd, *Assembly Themes* (Mowbray).

R.H. Lloyd, *More Assembly Services* (Mowbray).

R.H. Lloyd, *Services for Betweenagers* (Mowbray).

R.H. Lloyd, *All Assembly Services* (Religious Education Press).

Nancy Martin, *Prayers for Children and Young People* (Hodder & Stoughton).

General Books related to Families and Family Services

Michael Botting (ed.), *For All the Family*—80 illustrated talks for Family Services (Kingsway).

Michael Botting (ed.), *More for All the Family*—90 illustrated talks for Family Services (Kingsway).

Michael Botting (ed.), *Teaching the Families*—Revised (Kingsway).

Maggie Durran, *All Age Worship* (Angel Press).

Leslie J. Francis, *Making Contact* (Collins).

Peter Graystone, *Help! There's a Child in My Church* (Scripture Union).

* Ronald Jasper, *Worship and the Child* (SPCK).

Jane Keiller, *Praying with Children in the Home* (Grove Spirituality 42).

* Paul Marston, *God and the Family* (Kingsway).

* Methodist Youth Department, *Together in Church*.

Mothers' Union, *Let's Have Children in Church*.

Brian Ogden and Eveline Wyatt, *Christian Family Festivals* (CIO).

Michael Perham (ed.), *Liturgy for a New Century* (SPCK/Alcuin Club).

Kenneth Stevenson, *Family Services* (Alcuin Club Manual No. 3/SPCK).

Judith Wigley, *Under Fives & Their Families* (CPAS).

Reports by the General Synod of the Church of England

Children in the Way (NS/CHP).

All God's Children? (NS/CHP).

The Worship of the Church As It Approaches the Third Millennium (CHP).

Acknowledgements

Collects and other material from *The Alternative Service Book*, 1980 are reproduced by permission of The Central Board of Finance of the Church of England.

Material from *Church Family Worship* is used by kind permission of Jubilate Hymns and Hodder & Stoughton.

Hodder & Stoughton, publishers of *Contemporary Parish Prayers* edited by Frank Colquhoun, for prayers of mine nos. 104, 107, 110, 113, 116, 119, 122, 249, 364 and 549. Also for other prayers from their book as acknowledged in the text of this book.

Hodder & Stoughton, publishers of *New Parish Prayers* edited by Frank Colquhoun, for prayers of mine nos. 139, 303, 322, 446, 459, 464, 479, 492, 502 and 518. Also for other prayers from their book as acknowledged in the text of this book.

Prayers for Children and Young People, 1975, an anthology by Nancy Martin, published by Hodder & Stoughton. Permission to reprint some of the prayers from this book has been kindly given by Mrs Martin and her family.

Prayers by Zinnia Symonds (nee Bryan) are taken from *Let's Talk to God*, published by Scripture Union, 1969.

Victor Gollancz Limited, the original publishers of *Prayers and Graces*, 1944, collected by the late Allen M. Laing, have been unable to discover who holds the copyright of the graces marked * used in Section 2 Chapter 5. Should any reader be able to inform me of the copyright holder I will gladly make an acknowledgement in any future publication of this book.

In the late sixties clergy from over a hundred churches sent me copies of family services they used or had devised—or both. These were to help Canon Michael Cole and me to draw up what proved to be a nationally accepted *Family Service*. The result of our labours was eventually published by the Church Pastoral Aid Society. I have used some of the prayers contained in those family services that I received, some adapted. I have received permission to print from the present leaders of the churches concerned, who do not necessarily know the identity of the original authors. If any authors recognise their work and inform me, I will see that they are acknowledged in any future publications of this book. The *Family Service* mentioned above was eventually incorporated in the book *Family Worship*, first published by CPAS in 1971. I hold the copyright of the prayers contained in that book.

Further information about prayers, where details in the text are insufficient:

37. Part of a prayer by Gordon Bates, Bishop of Whitby.
83. Published by SPCK.
85. From *Prayer for Children and Young People*, compiled by Nancy Martin and published by Hodder & Stoughton.
95. Permission granted by the Methodist Church Division of Education and Youth, 2 Chester House, Pages Lane, London N10 1PZ.
112. Edited by Caryl Micklem, SCM Press 1967 to be used in litanised form.
145. Week of Prayer for Christian Unity 1971. Copyright sought.
152. Copyright sought.
156. Week of Prayer for Christian Unity 1971. Copyright sought.
169. Copyright permission granted for use in *Family Worship*. For this book copyright being sought.
189. Published by John Paul, The Preacher's Press, Charlton House, Hunslett Road, Leeds LS10 1JW. Copyright sought.
326. From *First Prayers* published by The Lutterworth Press, P.O. Box 60, Cambridge CB1 2NT. This prayer may not be reproduced without special permission from the publishers.
329. Copyright permission granted by The National Society for Promoting Religious Education.
335. Reprinted by permission of Oxford University Press.
365. Copyright granted by Highway Press (CMS).
379. Copyright granted by the General Hospital, Nottingham.
403. Copyright granted by Highway Press (CMS).

Subject Index